FRILANDS MUSEET

PETER MICHELSEN

FRILANDS MUSEET

The Danish Museum Village at Sorgenfri

A HISTORY OF AN OPEN-AIR MUSEUM AND ITS OLD BUILDINGS

THE NATIONAL MUSEUM OF DENMARK

*This book is due to the initiative of the Savings Bank
Sparekassen for Lyngby og Omegns Foundation, and its
publication has been made possible by a grant to
the National Museum on the occasion of the 75th
anniversary of the Savings Bank on 29th September 1973.*

Colour photographs by Lennart Larsen
Translation by Jean Olsen

Contents

Preface

Frilandsmuseet owes a debt of gratitude to *Sparekassen for Lyngby og Omegn* for the publication of this book to mark the 75th anniversary of the Savings Bank. A lasting tribute was desired to commemorate the event, and what is more lasting than a book? The chosen subject had to represent a common bond for the entire area served by the Savings Bank. And there is no doubt that the museum park with its old farmsteads and cottages is felt as such by those who live in this extensive green belt district. Frilandsmuseet is also a nation-wide institution in the sense that its contents reflect the background of the greater part of the Danish population. The subject, in other words, has a range so wide that a book about it is a worthy way in which to celebrate the 75th anniversary of a public utility such as a savings bank.

When the idea arose of celebrating the anniversary by making a grant to the National Museum towards the publication of this volume, it was largely inspired by a book about another Danish open-air museum published shortly before: Bo Bramsen's description of the Old Town Museum in Århus commissioned by *Århus Oliefabrik A/S* on the occasion of its centenary in 1971. By following the example set by this book in format and style, it is the hope of the Savings Bank and the National Museum that these books will be the first of a series of publications about noteworthy places in Denmark. And that perhaps other firms and institutions will follow suit and commemorate anniversaries and similar occasions by offering financial support towards the publication of books like these which normally exceeds the means of cultural institutions alone.

At Frilandsmuseet the lack of a general description of the museum's history and old buildings has long been felt. It was therefore with great pleasure that the author at once supported the idea of publishing a book of this kind, especially as it proved possible to print an edition large enough to ensure a reasonably widespread distribution. This was because the National Museum's Publications Department undertook to produce the book and to bear the financial risk of publishing it in both Danish and English.

Some readers of the book are neighbours of the museum who know every plot and its surroundings in the museum park. But the readership will also include people with a general interest, living in distant countries with no close knowledge of the culture of Northern Europe and unacquainted with local history in Denmark: the land reforms, for example, at the close of the 18th century, and the reorganisation of agriculture in the 1880's. It is difficult, though, to pay equal attention to every type of reader and to find the right balance between local colour and a general historical context.

Writing about Frilandsmuseet presents many difficulties common to works of this kind. For an account of the history of an institution will often contain trivia of interest only to a narrow circle of readers. But other facets may be seen in the light of the history of ideas and research, and as

7

such they are of general interest. When describing a homestead, the very individual history of the building and its occupants has to be combined with information about the kind of homestead in general and which group of the rural population lived there.

Taking photographs at Frilandsmuseet also poses problems. It is easy to fall for the temptation to concentrate on what is aesthetically pleasing. Colour photography tends to record the bright and colourful, while black and white photography shows the marked contrast between light and shade, and tones of grey.

These difficulties reflect the problems of arranging an open-air museum. Research ensures that the criteria for choosing exhibits are as correct as possible. Where, then, is the sombre social realism we may expect? The fact is that much of what should be portrayed in black and grey has long since disappeared. What has not survived is not seen, thus causing a simplification which needs comment. This entire book is a commentary. It is not intended to replace the experience of independent observation during a visit to Frilandsmuseet or a similar museum elsewhere, for museums should not only be read about – they must be seen.

Frilandsmuseet, March 1973.
PETER MICHELSEN

The History of Frilandsmuseet

The Conception of an Open-Air Museum

If, as far as *Frilandsmuseet* the Open-Air Museum is concerned, one man were to be pointed out as the first to conceive the idea of the undertaking in its earliest form, and the driving force behind its realisation, his name must be Bernhard Olsen, the founder of the museum. However, it was not an isolated idea conceived in the mind of one man, but as so often is the case, it sprang from a background of many contemporary factors.

One of the factors behind the conception of this museum of old rural dwellings was the position of the peasantry in Denmark during the second half of the 19th century, and its steadily increasing influence, both political and on Danish society as a whole. It cannot be denied, though, that a fair portion of rustic romanticism also existed during this period. On the other hand, a certain measure of enlightenment among the farming population, based on the teaching at village schools and folk high-schools, can well have resulted in an increased historical awareness. But enlightenment served the cause of progress, first and foremost, by preparing the way for radical changes in the entire material culture of the peasantry in connection with the reorganisation of Danish farming and marketing of produce in the 1880's, when co-operative dairies and the co-operative movement as a whole got underway. This cultural upheaval caused the relics of former times to be ruthlessly swept away, and gave the folk museums

The farmstead from Sønder Sejerslev stands out sharply in the winter sunshine. There is not as yet much to soften its façade as the garden has not had many years to grow in. But lime trees grow in the same position in front of the windows of the living-room as those on the farmstead's native site.

and open-air museums formed at this period a mission to fulfil.

At the same time, the study of folk culture split away from the main body of historical research, the first major work to represent it being Troels-Lund's *Dagligt Liv i Norden* (Daily Life in the North). During these years, too, the research into rural building traditions was begun which led to a fine book on the farmhouses of Schleswig by R. Mejborg published in 1892. It was no coincidence that the rural buildings of North Schleswig were the subject of this painstaking study. For national feelings after the border war in 1864 played a role in the choice of subject for historical research, and possibly in the germination of a true folk history. History was no longer solely about kings, nobles and wars, but also about ordinary people and their daily lives. It was therefore not surprising that museums were formed, the collections of which were centred about the peasantry and those associated with it in bygone days.

Part of the background for the founding of Frilandsmuseet at the close of the 19th century was the formation of a number of folk museums some years earlier. In this context, particular mention should be made of Nordiska Museet in Stockholm founded by Artur Hazelius in 1873. For this museum greatly influenced the general development of museums throughout Europe, and it was an important source of inspiration for the Danish Folk Museum which was opened to the public in Copenhagen in 1885.

A characteristic feature of the period, too, is the fact that the impetus was partly due to an exhibition. The latter half of the 19th century was an era of great exhibitions. The growth of industry was the hallmark of these exhibitions, demonstrating through them in optimistic terms the delights of progress; nevertheless, farming was also a dominant theme of many. The

11

enormous quantity of exhibits gathered together often formed the nucleus of a new museum. The founding of the Victoria and Albert Museum in London, for example, was partly a result of the world exhibition at the Crystal Palace in 1851.

It was at the world fair in Paris in 1878 that Bernhard Olsen met Artur Hazelius. The founder of Nordiska Museet had arranged a historical display in the Swedish section of this exhibition. Here, some old farmhouse interiors were exhibited, very much as stage sets with one side open towards the audience. There was also a Dutch interior at the exhibition, but this was a real room with four walls, enabling visitors to experience the interior by walking into the room. The idea appealed to Bernhard Olsen, for he felt that the atmosphere of the past was conveyed far more intensely by these means than by the slightly theatrical Swedish tableaux.

He was, on the other hand, a man well qualified to judge something reminiscent of the theatre. He had begun his career by training as a graphic artist, and became a popular illustrator. Bernhard Olsen's association with the world of amusements in Copenhagen developed at an early date. The highlight of this phase of his career were the many years he spent as director of Tivoli, while also working on commissions for the Casino and the Royal Theatre. Both in Tivoli and the theatres he was concerned with costumes and stage decoration – activities demanding some insight into history and tradition. However, history and theatre fused when Bernhard Olsen created the Panoptikon waxworks in Copenhagen, where visitors could view historical and contemporary figures and scenes, a form of entertainment highly favoured both then and later. The Panoptikon opened in 1885 in a house in Vesterbrogade, near the main station, and a week later the Danish Folk

Museum was inaugurated in the same building. At the age of forty-nine, Bernhard Olsen now concentrated on running this museum, the basic ideas for which had been laid by him a number of years earlier in conjunction with all his other activities.

The immediate point of departure behind the founding of the Danish Folk Museum was the exhibition of art and industry held in Copenhagen in 1879, and the historical theme was conspicuous in its arrangement. The display of exhibits devoted to folk culture was undertaken by Bernhard Olsen. He moved some old farmhouse interiors complete with panelling and furniture to the exhibition. In these interiors he arranged waxworks figures clad in the colourful folk costumes – which were then falling out of use – from various parts of the country.

This exhibition was a great success, and the rural interiors in particular won public acclaim. It soon became clear that these exhibits ought to form the nucleus of a museum. In this, Bernhard Olsen received the understanding and support of J.J.A. Worsaae, the archeologist, a leading figure in museum circles at that time. Worsaae had been chairman of the exhibition committee, and he now became chairman of the committee formed to launch the Folk Museum. His influence was considerable, and his interests were by no means limited to archeology. Apart from leading the Oldnordisk Museum, he was also keeper of the Royal Collection at Rosenborg Castle, and therefore no stranger to the type of museum display based on naturally furnished settings.

The backbone of the Danish Folk Museum were the furnished rooms from the exhibition, and these had been supplemented in the years that followed. The museum was primarily based on the interior principle. Rooms were to be equipped with the furniture and belongings that had been part of them when they were lived in. That this principle could not be followed absolutely literally is another matter. For lack of space was a pressing problem at the museum from the beginning, and exhibits from other displays tended to spread into the interiors.

Moreover, when the aim is to give visitors an impression of daily life in the past, a row of interiors from various parts of the country is not quite sufficient. The interiors are torn from both the building to which they belong, and the other rooms within it. Bernhard Olsen found this unsatisfactory, and he later intimated that, when working on the exhibition, he had toyed with the thought of moving entire buildings. He felt that some of the very old buildings he had seen during his travels contained some ancient building traditions, which no coming Folk Museum should be without.

What Bernhard Olsen called the natural consequence of a display of interiors, namely a museum of buildings, did not come to anything at this period. Immediately after opening in 1885, the position of the Folk Museum was presumably weakened by the death of Worsaae, and a number of years passed before the idea of an open-air museum could be realised. In the meantime open-air museums were underway elsewhere in Scandinavia, and when the new department of the Folk Museum became a reality in 1897, it was not therefore the first open-air museum.

That kindred museums were established in close succession in Scandinavia during these years was not purely coincidental, for they sprang from much the same school of thought. On the other hand, it is doubtful how much the earlier tentative efforts to move old buildings and to collect them in groups have meant for the creation of open-air museums.

Attention has been drawn to the fact that the Swiss writer von Bonstetten sug-

This photograph of Bernhard Olsen was presumably taken sometime between c. 1897 and c. 1909. It was during this period that he was most intensely engaged with the founding and organisation of Frilandsmuseet.

gested something on the lines of an open-air museum during his sojourn in Denmark in the 1790's. He considered that the statues of Norwegian peasants in folk costume displayed in the royal park at Fredensborg Castle should also be accompanied by their dwellings – complete with furniture and tools. He was obviously of the opinion that this would be educational in a variety of ways.

Although von Bonstetten's suggestion was based on some sort of practical aim, it nevertheless reflected the ideas and taste of the period for romantic gardens. In these gardens one of the elements of surprise during a stroll could well be a rustic cottage. Here, those of high birth enacted the simple life of their inferiors in the pastoral idyll that was much in favour.

13

All are familiar with the gardens of the Petit Trianon and Chantilly in France, and these had their imitations elsewhere in Europe. However, the fashion reached our northern latitudes in a very modest form, and it is not very conceivable that this movement had much connection with the later creation of open-air museums.

The same may be said of the moving of individual buildings which occurred here and there during the 19th century. It was perhaps an expression of a true interest in old building traditions, but not part of a systematic salvage action. If a Norwegian stave-church could end in Silesia it simply illustrated the capacity of a prince to accomplish a whim of this nature, yet there are undoubtedly instances in which old buildings were saved from destruction by removal.

The first national move and more purposeful effort to save representative examples of old buildings and exhibit them collectively as an open-air museum crystallised in Norway. A stave-church provided the occasion, it was acquired in 1881 and moved to Bygdøy near Oslo, where it was soon joined by other old buildings. The union of Sweden and Norway was then ruled by King Oscar II who had a royal farm in Bygdøy, and this monarch played a leading role in establishing the museum of buildings here which became incorporated with the Norwegian Folk Museum founded later.

But before embarking on a description of the succession of early open-air museums formed in Scandinavia during this great initial period, a brief European interlude is called for. For example, at the world fair in Vienna in 1873 copies of a group of old farmhouses were exhibited, yet it is unlikely that this display had any long-lasting impact, unless the theory that it had some influence on Artur Hazelius is correct. In Amsterdam a colonial exhibition was held in 1883, and a few houses

from Indonesia were re-erected on the site of the exhibition. They were transferred to Leiden in 1885, and comprised a small open-air section of the ethnographic museum there until 1903, when a storm destroyed these houses from a distant culture. Finally, mention should be made of a French exhibit in 1889 composed of a collection of full-scale houses and dwellings to demonstrate how a variety of different races lived.

In Stockholm the Nordiska Museet, founded in 1873, was enlarged by an open-air department situated in Skansen in 1891. This was the first really well-known open-air museum, and destined to play an important role as a recreative centre in the heart of the city for Stockholmers. In 1892 the folk museum of Lund was opened, better known by the name "Kulturen", also with an open-air section. In Norway, too, the first house was bought for the Sandvig Collection in Lillehammer in 1894, although it was not moved to Maihaugen until some years later.

This, then, completes the picture of the open-air museum movement at the time that Bernhard Olsen ultimately succeeded in realising his early ambitions of moving entire houses to a museum. There had been much talk in the intermediate years about finding a solution to the space problems experienced by museums in Copenhagen. The Danish Folk Museum's quarters in the Panoptikon building were considered a temporary measure, as its collections were a chronological continuation of those of the National Museum. There were plans, therefore, of amalgamating the two museums, as well as of moving the National Museum from Prinsens Palæ to the parade ground of Rosenborg Castle. This is the reason why Denmark's first open-air museum was situated in the royal gardens of Rosenborg, known as Kongens Have.

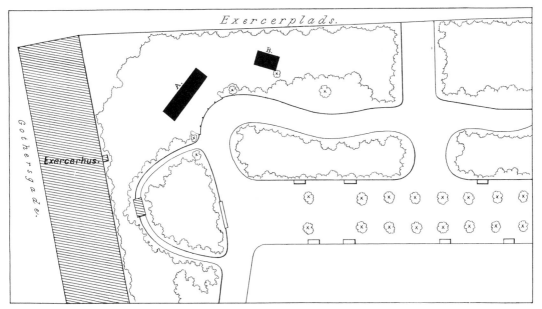

Plan showing part of what was then called "the pleasure gardens of Rosenborg" – Kongens Have the royal gardens in Copenhagen. The nucleus of Frilandsmuseet: (A) the dwelling-house of the Halland farmstead and (B) the loft house from Småland were re-erected here in a corner of the gardens with the parade ground on one side, and on the other the drill-house (since demolished) along Gothersgade. The plan presumably dates from 1897 or shortly after.

The Museum of Buildings in Kongens Have

The open-air department of the Folk Museum was inaugurated in 1897 in Kongens Have, the royal gardens. It was a very modest place indeed, and conditions were such that it remained a curiously forgotten little museum for the short period of its existence in Kongens Have.

The position chosen for the museum of old buildings was in the south-westerly corner of the royal gardens. It appears to have been a dank, overgrown corner with the parade ground on one side, and view to the thoroughfare of Gothersgade blocked by a drill-house (later demolished). If the plans for moving the National Museum and the Folk Museum to the parade ground had materialised, the old buildings of the open-air section would have adjoined the wing containing the historic collections. But as it transpired, these plans were finally shelved shortly after the founding of the little open-air section, whose duration in Kongens Have was only a curious intermezzo in the early history of Frilandsmuseet.

The two buildings moved to Kongens Have, however, can tell us a considerable amount about the thoughts which lay behind the creation of a museum of this kind. Bernhard Olsen had published, moreover, a little guide to the old buildings in which he explained the background for this rural note in the middle of a city park.

Bernhard Olsen clearly meant that because of the innate conservatism of the rural population, it was possible to gain an impression of living conditions in fact far older than the actual age of the houses. He expressed it thus: "The homes of the peasantry have always been imitations of the interiors of large farmsteads and later, of town houses. Because of this they often

15

give a good idea of cultural patterns which have long ceased to exist in their original setting. By studying the dwellings of the peasantry in two areas, we can still gain an impression of indoor life in far distant times, indeed the early Middle Ages. But this can only be done in areas which no longer belong to Denmark, namely South Schleswig and the Swedish provinces east of the Sound – Halland, Scania and Blekinge".

This demonstrates that it was not romantic nationalism which caused Bernhard Olsen to search beyond Danish frontiers for the first buildings for his museum. Neither was it a desire to have the erstwhile Danish territories represented in the museum. The reason for the choice was that in these regions particularly early building traditions could be encoun-

tered, which had disappeared from the cultural heartland of Denmark.

Both the old buildings re-erected in Kongens Have came from the other side of the Sound. One was called the Halland dwelling and consisted of a dwelling-house in three sections; farm buildings were added later and it is now a complete Halland farmstead. In this dwelling-house Bernhard Olsen felt he had found something that satisfied his criteria of true age. Of the three sections, the two end houses on each side of the lower house in the middle are later additions. It was the house in the middle which, when taken alone "brings to mind a house of great antiquity that could be built like this as long as there was a plentiful supply of fine timber in the vicinity". Bernhard Olsen did not doubt that a glance at the thick

16

timbers of the lower house "would convince all that it goes back to the time Halland was Danish". He visualised what it must have looked like originally: "In those days chimneys were unknown. A fire burned in an open hearth, like those to be found not long ago in Norway, the Skaw and Schleswig south of Danevirke. Smoke seeped out through a smoke hole or louver in the roof. In those days, too, three walls of the room were lined with benches, and on these the servants slept. The place of honour was the gable bench, and here slept the farmer and his wife".

The other building in Kongens Have was a loft house from Småland some distance north of the Blekinge border, possibly the idea originally was to find a building to represent the Blekinge region. But the deciding factor was to find and acquire a two-storied building of this kind with an outside ladder leading to a balcony. It was in any event impossible to find in Denmark, for this type of building had long since disappeared. That loft houses had existed here Bernhard Olsen did not doubt, he was also fairly certain what they had looked like because in his opinion "evidence can be found in the countries of Scandinavia, with the exception of Iceland, to show that these houses were all built alike in the late medieval period". Although aware that the loft house in question was not conceivably more than two hundred years old, he maintained that the manner in which it was built had its roots in the late Middle Ages. It was feasible to compare this storehouse with the high loft mentioned in folk songs, best known in its role as a ladies' bower.

These two buildings, then, were the only two acquired for the open-air museum in Kongens Have. However, from the point of view of museum display, it is interesting to note that the interior principle to which Bernhard Olsen adhered when planning the Danish Folk Museum, was not put into full effect in the Kongens Have museum. The loft house from Småland was not equipped until a much later date with the belongings ordinarily to be found in buildings of this kind. When situated in Kongens Have it contained the usual type of museum display to illuminate the conditions of the farming community in the era of the open field system. A landscape painting was also exhibited, which Bernhard Olsen had commissioned, it was a copy of a photograph showing the original setting of the museum's Halland house.

The Museum of Buildings in Kongens Lyngby

Already shortly after opening the museum in Kongens Have it must have been obvious to all that there was no future for an open-air museum here. Plans for a concentration of museums near Rosenborg Castle had been abandoned, and it was decided that the Folk Museum and National Museum should amalgamate in Prinsens Palæ which was to be enlarged at some future date. The National Museum is still in this mid-18th century palace (since enlarged). The situation, then, was that the Folk Museum and its open-air section could not be combined after all, and the latter need not remain in a corner of a public park where the chances for expansion were slight. Another site with sufficient acreage had to be found.

The location of the Open-Air Museum was decided when a plot of land was purchased north of the park belonging to Sorgenfri Castle, a royal residence near Lyngby. Prior to this transaction several possibilities had been discussed, particu-

larly sites in or near any of the parks in
Copenhagen. These proposals were resur-
rected once more in the ensuing years
during continual discussions about the
future of the National Museum. The desire to unite the Folk Museum with its
open-air section brought the location under discussion again, as late as the 1920's
in fact, just prior to the large-scale extension to Prinsens Palæ. During the course of the years, however, Frilandsmuseet
– the Open-Air Museum – had grown so
much that thoughts about moving it were
obviously unreasonable.

*Plan showing the plot north of the gardens and grounds
of Sorgenfri Castle to which the museum moved in 1901.
It gives a personal touch to Bernhard Olsen's activities
in 1899 and 1900. In the margin of the map the founder
of the museum asks for the corners of the Näs twin
farmstead to be drawn in. The result can be seen at the
top of the map. The site of the Ostenfeld farmstead
(centre) also appears to have been decided for Bernhard
Olsen requests its position to be marked out in the field.
The planting of bushes etc. on the slopes is indicated in
watercolour with additional notes, for example "280
Sweetbriar" for the Rose Path.*

The choice fell on the land north of
Lyngby for a number of reasons. The town
of Lyngby at that time barely extended

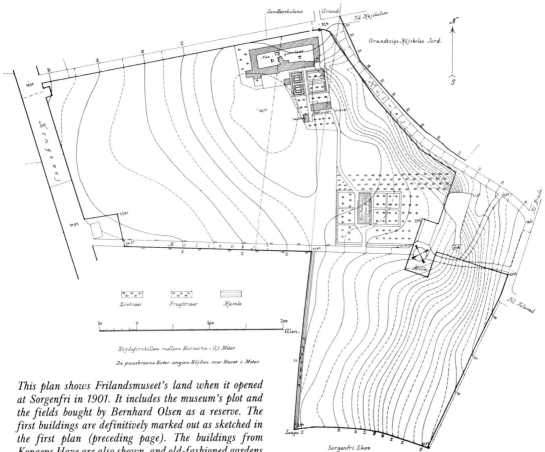

This plan shows Frilandsmuseet's land when it opened at Sorgenfri in 1901. It includes the museum's plot and the fields bought by Bernhard Olsen as a reserve. The first buildings are definitively marked out as sketched in the first plan (preceding page). The buildings from Kongens Have are also shown, and old-fashioned gardens are drawn round all the buildings. The indentation is the site of Fuglevad windmill still privately owned at that time. Close by is a gravel pit later transformed to a dancing green. The plan presumably dates from 1900 or 1901.

as far as the grounds of Sorgenfri Castle. There had originally been open farming country north of the extensive royal park, chiefly belonging to the village of Virum. By the highway, Kongevejen, there was a single farmstead and one or two houses, otherwise only the large Dutch windmill which towered over the fields above Fuglevad. To the east our gaze would be halted by great oak trees on the slopes leading down to the river Mølleåen. However, the landscape changed in the course of the last half of the 19th century. Lyngby Agricultural College was built in the middle of the fields, the foundation stone was laid in 1867. In close association with this college and in its immediate vicinity more buildings were erected in 1897 for a folk high-school called Grundtvig's High-School. The area thus became an educational centre for young people where a vocational agricultural training was part of the curriculum. Some of the land was cultivated as experimental fields partly by the State, partly by the Danish association of co-operative societies F.D.B. But as is so often the case in a folk high-school milieu, the economics of agriculture formed a synthesis with intellectual processes and with a certain measure of

The Rose Path led from the gardens of Sorgenfri Castle to the gate into the museum. To the right of the path can be seen the Ostenfeld farmstead, the earlier Museum of Agriculture, and the main building of the folk high-school. Photographed shortly after 1901.

historical awareness. This found expression, for example, in the founding of the Museum of Agriculture, a neighbour to the Lyngby Agricultural College. It was housed in a wooden exhibition building moved from the great exhibition in Copenhagen in 1888. This building later burned down, but fortunately the collections of the Museum of Agriculture had long since been moved to the large brick-built museum building erected in 1915 on the other side of Kongevejen, beside the solitary farmstead of Virumgård which had been acquired by the State.

There were, then, a number of excellent reasons why the district north of Sorgenfri Castle's park was chosen for the Open-Air Museum. It was admittedly some distance from Copenhagen and rather out of the way. However, the new railway project from Lyngby to Vedbæk would outweigh this disadvantage to some ex-

tent. The construction of the railway was agreed upon in 1896; nowadays the railway only extends as far as Nærum. But it was presumably an important factor in deciding whether such a distant location could be chosen for a museum. Visitors would be able to get off the train at Fuglevad – just below the colleges and the field chosen for the museum. The prospect of keen young men who flocked to the colleges and centre of experimental agriculture each year becoming a natural museum public as Bernhard Olsen pointed out, presumably tipped the scales in favour of the site.

There had been some contact between the circles close to the Folk Museum and the agricultural circles in Lyngby as early

20

View to the south from approximately the same position as where the Halland farmstead now stands. On the other side of the sunken road is the Fuglevad windmill, and beside it an outbuilding with clay walls which to the chagrin of later museum staff was pulled down shortly afterwards. To the extreme right is the newly re-erected Ostenfeld farmstead, whose half-timbered gable is set off by the dark fringe of the woods. Photographed in 1901 or shortly after.

as 1897, i.e. when the open-air section was inaugurated in Kongens Have. The Folk Museum was offered the lease of a plot in Lyngby but it was far too small. The land purchased finally in 1899 was only approximately six acres, but with considerable foresight Bernhard Olsen bought twice as much himself, in order to ensure that the museum would have enough land yet at the same time avoiding overtaxing its slender finances. This reserve land was leased for experimental farming, thus safeguarding the rural qualities of the landscape closest to the museum.

When the museum of buildings was opened on 24th June 1901, it was already notably bigger than it had been in Kongens Have. Apart from the two old buildings which had been transferred from the gardens of Rosenborg Castle, there were two additional farmsteads which, to this day, are among the largest and most noteworthy in the Open-Air Museum. One was the farmstead from Ostenfeld in South Schleswig and the other was the twin farmstead from West Göinge in Scania, Sweden.

Bernhard Olsen still found his old buildings beyond Danish territory, and he cannot be entirely absolved from a certain emotional attachment in his choice of buildings from lost Danish possessions. He had taken part in the war of 1864. In his description of the Ostenfeld farmstead he wrote: "Many will still recall their service as soldiers in our army in 1863 when billeted in Hytten county, how

21

new and strange these farmhouses seemed to us, and the life lived in them". This was not just a comment to the fact that here the Danish army was about to leave the region of Scandinavian building traditions, and had encountered the most northerly representatives of an entirely foreign impulse. His emotional involvement is very apparent in the association of his thoughts, because after describing the dark figures grouped about the flaming hearth in these strange buildings he springs abruptly to the other end of Denmark: "It gave the same vivid impression as when on Midsummer's Eve one stands by the Sound and sees the glow of bonfires along our coast and across the water in Scania – as far as the eye can see".

The official, scholarly reason governing the choice of old buildings for the Open-Air Museum was a different one, it was simply that some extremely old-fashioned types of building still survived in former Danish territory which were no longer to be found in Denmark. A characteristic view current at the close of the 19th century and beginning of the present century was that the buildings in the museum should illustrate an evolutionary sequence. This was in keeping with the evolutionary teaching in the field of natural science, which in turn marked the humanist research of the period and influenced the approach to general concepts such as culture.

The first link in Bernhard Olsen's evolutionary sequence was the farmstead from Ostenfeld, which he classified, without hesitation as a house-type with roots in antiquity. The absence of a chimney was to him the key piece of evidence – the inhabitants of the farmstead kept to the open hearth in one end of the main nave of the building. The custom of man and beast living in the same room was also considered a relic from prehistoric times. This old-fashioned tradition of a

large barn-like interior housing both man and beast was common throughout North Germany at the turn of the century. Obviously it is barely conceivable that any farmhouses of this type had not been given additional rooms in the course of time. Bernhard Olsen was naturally fully aware of the fact. Therefore, the two earliest additional living quarters for the farmer and his family were also moved to the museum, although they were not as venerable from the point of view of age as the main hall, which was over two hundred years old when acquired by the museum. The outbuildings of more recent date, on the other hand, which had been used in conjunction with the dwelling-house, were not included. This was in full agreement with the principles normally applied to the restoration of old buildings at that period, by which a building was re-created in its earlier form. The result was a pedagogical simplification in many ways, designed to throw the criteria by which it was chosen into sharp relief.

The second link of the evolutionary sequence visualised by Bernhard Olsen was embodied in a farmhouse from North Schleswig. The most significant characteristic of this phase being that although man and beast still lived under the same roof, they no longer shared the same room – the byre and stables were separated from the living quarters by a partition wall. A farmstead of this kind, as a representative of what Bernhard Olsen considered the medieval stage, had not been acquired by the museum when it opened in Lyngby in 1901. The third phase, however, was already represented in the first open-air collection in Kongens Have: namely the Halland house in which cattle no longer sheltered under the same roof as the farmer.

The fourth phase in the sequence comprising Bernhard Olsen's integral evolutionary whole was what he believed to

To begin with Frilandsmuseet stood in a bare field. All the trees and bushes planted during the first years in Sorgenfri have not yet altered the landscape. In the foreground is the west side of the Näs twin farmstead. To the right is the Halland dwelling-house, the loft house, and the Ostenfeld farmstead, behind the roof of which looms the Fuglevad windmill. Photographed shortly after the museum opened in Lyngby, 1901 or 1902.

represent the fully developed farmhouse of South Scandinavia: the twin farmstead from Göinge in Scania which had been acquired by the Open-Air Museum and re-erected in time for the opening in 1901. As everyone can judge for themselves to this day, it is a large impressive farm consisting of two steadings built for two neighbouring occupiers. In this case, too, buildings of considerable age had been acquired, and at least part of them goes back to the latter half of the 17th century. In the same way as the house from Halland, the dwelling-houses in the Scanian twin farmstead are clearly divided into a

collection of heated and unheated small "houses". The similarity goes one step further, in that both in the Halland farmhouse and the twin farmstead chimneys of ancient and interesting types are to be found – in all likelihood the successors of the even older chimneyless stadium.

With an optimism that seems to be characteristic of the close of the 19th century, Bernhard Olsen believed that his evolutionary sequence embraced all conceivable major categories in the evolution of the house. In those days, however, no particular humility was felt by the possibility of future research yielding material that would change basic concepts. This was also the case in the study of folk culture, when old rural buildings were the object of research, and this in turn decided which buildings should be moved to the new Open-Air Museum – "if future generations add more buildings, variations of these types must be chosen".

The two large newly acquired farmsteads were extremely well-equipped when the museum opened. They were furnished with belongings acquired from their native region, and as far as possible the interiors were arranged in a natural way, although this was difficult to accomplish with complete consistency because the aim was to show such exceedingly old-fashioned interiors. The illusion of everyday life in the old buildings in the past was undoubtedly shattered once or twice. The sale of tickets and guide-books in the Ostenfeld farmhouse was not perhaps too disturbing, as no entrance to the museum had yet been built. A cupboard in the same farm was turned into a lavatory for those visiting the museum. Display principles in the Scanian farmstead went from one extreme to the other – the interior display was adopted in its most excessive form in one of the rooms, in which a table was laid for a feast complete with pig's head and other delicacies. While the outbuildings, on the other hand, contained the usual systematic display of objects. The exhibits here belonged to the Museum of Agriculture which had grown so quickly that it could no longer accommodate all its acquisitions in its first premises beside Frilandsmuseet.

Something which deeply interested Bernhard Olsen was the setting in which these old buildings were to be exhibited, intended as they were, to show the history of homes as well as rural life in the era before the great agricultural reforms. The earliest photographs of the museum show that the buildings stood in bare fields. This state of affairs, however, did not last long. Bernhard Olsen declares that he will "surround the farmsteads with hop gardens and flower gardens, kitchen gardens and orchards, as well as trees". Some of the rose bushes he planted by the Scanian farm still survive. His ideas particularly left their mark on the planting of the sloping area, west of the old sunken road, leading down to the river Mølleåen at Fuglevad. It was on the perimeter of the land originally owned by Frilandsmuseet, and here the founder of the museum wanted "oaks rising above an underbrush of hawthorn, hazel and juniper as a haven for song-birds", and elsewhere he instructed that "trees and bushes be planted of native species in great variety to grow into a natural boundary". Some of these plans were realised with the help of cheap labour. For example, one or two boys from Brede children's home down at the end of the old track came and sowed acorns and woodland seeds in the furrows ploughed along the slopes. The fine oak trees grouped in the terrain around the central clearing and kiosk are the result.

The First Decades in Lyngby

Frilandsmuseet could be reached by various means. Most people probably took the train to Lyngby, changed there to the Vedbæk line and alighted at Fuglevad. One could also walk to the museum from Lyngby, although it was perhaps a little dull trudging along the Elsinore highway as the main road Kongevejen, was then called. By foot the most attractive route was to walk through the gardens and grounds of Sorgenfri Castle by the winding paths along the banks of the Mølleåen. If the road seemed long and it was hot and dusty, cooling soft drinks could be bought from a woman who used to stand by the grotto on the slope below the castle.

In those days there was no broad road to cross, separating the northerly end of the castle park from the museum – the road was built much later. Visitors could walk along an idyllic path called the Rose Path which had been specially laid out, the big windmill stood diagonally to the right – if it were possible to see over the rosebushes bordering the entire length of the path. In the distance could be glimpsed the buildings of the Agricultural College up on the hill as one approached the entrance to Frilandsmuseet.

During the first few years, visitors simply entered the museum's grounds at the Östenfeld farmstead. However, a proper entrance was soon established just beside this farmstead. It faced onto Museumsvej, a road which still exists but now within the museum. In those days it was a side road to Kongevejen and led straight down to the Fuglevad windmill which stood just beyond the museum boundary. The windmill was still privately owned at that time and working normally.

Only a few years after the museum opened the entrance was arranged so that visitors had to pass between two marble lions – the same lions which stand in front of the present entrance. By the old entrance, though, they stood much closer together leaving just enough room for a narrow gate between their plinths. These lions obviously had no connection with the contents of Frilandsmuseet, yet they were successful landmarks by the entrance and soon became a popular attraction for visitors to the museum and local children, who filled the lions' jaws with rose hips in the summer. The lions are not

25

There is a good view of the immediate surroundings at Frilandsmuseet from the platform of the Fuglevad windmill even though the Ostenfeld farmstead fills most of the picture. The farmstead then had quite a large garden. Behind is the entrance building and the old storehouse, at that time in 1908 only a year old.

particularly noble works of art, they are generally thought to be imitations of antique sculpture. They originally stood in the royal park at Fredensborg Castle.

Having passed the lions, the entrance building lay just beyond. It was a Norwegian plank-built house with a turf roof which had been transferred from the colonial exhibition in Copenhagen in 1905. In spite of its origin it was normally called Iceland House; this was because in addition to the usual functions of an entrance, it also housed a considerable collection of Icelandic folk art. Although these items had no real connection with Frilandsmuseet, they were exhibited here because the Danish Folk Museum suffered from a chronic shortage of space in Copenhagen.

This was also the reason why a large storage building was added to the back of the entrance pavilion in 1907. In this building visitors were confronted with an overwhelming miscellany of exhibits for which there was not enough room in the Folk Museum in Copenhagen. It must have been an exciting experience to explore these stores. Both buildings have long since been pulled down. However, at a time when the Open-Air Museum was not any larger and could be seen in its entirety during a short visit, it was to no disadvantage that there was more to look at, in rainy weather for example while waiting to return home by train.

During the course of the years more old buildings were re-erected in the museum park. To begin with buildings from regions outside Denmark continued to be selected, and the first addition after the

The 25th anniversary of the Folk Museum was celebrated in Sorgenfri. Colleagues and committee members, friends and relations assembled here. Bernhard Olsen (in the centre with white waistcoat) raises his glass in a toast.

museum opened in Lyngby represented the Faroe Islands. The word "represented" is used here very intentionally, because it cannot be said that this house "came from" the Faroe Islands. In any event, only partially, that is to say some decorative details and the furnishings. For the building itself was made for the colonial exhibition in Copenhagen in 1905. It was a copy of an old Faroese house, and when the exhibition closed it was taken over by the museum. The following year it could be seen with slight alterations and improvements at Frilandsmuseet in Lyngby. It remained here for many years until the museum built a Faroese hamlet with houses that really came from the Faroe Islands.

The so-called bath-house from Småland was acquired in 1908. It was actually a kiln with somewhat varied functions, but primarily a type with roots far back in time. It exemplified an interesting type of building, moreover, for it consisted of just one room which contained a form of stove not found in any other buildings in the museum.

The first acquisition to come from true Danish territory was a fisherman's hut from Nymindegab in West Jutland. It was brought to the museum in 1910, and was an example, salvaged at the last minute, of the small simple huts used in the past as temporary dwellings down on the shore by the peasants of West Jutland, who lived in them during the short fishing season. This hut also fitted into the sequence represented by the other buildings in the museum. It too was an expression of something extremely ancient and curi-

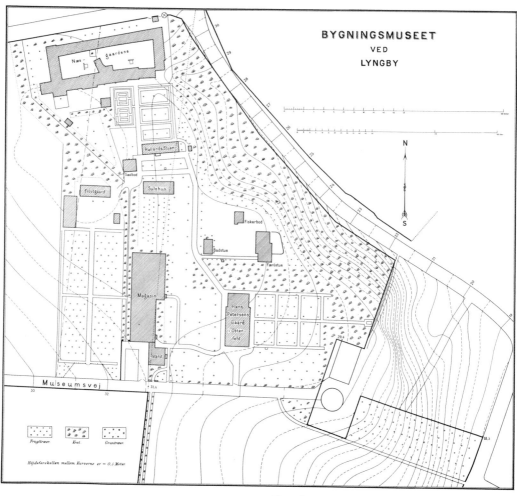

BYGNINGSMUSEET
VED
LYNGBY

Plan showing the growth of Frilandsmuseet by c. 1912. The Flovt house is plotted in as well as the first barn from Grønninghoved but not as yet the cottage from Fanø.

ous which not only visitors from Copenhagen, but also those from rural areas, must have studied with wonder. However, the fact that at long last a truly native building had been chosen for the museum, did not apparently indicate that the principles of selection had undergone any change. Yet the acquisitions of the years to follow revealed that a change was taking place. The buildings acquired during the second decade of the 20th century show that the museum's executive body had begun to adopt other criteria than earlier. There was an increasing awareness of the qualities of the more usual rural buildings in various regions of the country – that these were also worth moving to a museum.

As we have seen, Bernhard Olsen's choice of buildings was governed by a set concept. He attached importance to the way the interior of a building was arranged in relation to its occupants – both man and beast. Moreover, he considered the position and type of the hearth to be a key to the deeper understanding of the

The dwelling-house from Flovt was part of the North Schleswig farmstead – a composite collection of buildings with several examples of the Jutland bole construction. It has long since been removed to make room for the Zealand village.

building's history. However, his descriptions of the old houses gave much information as to the way they were built, and the various forms of construction adopted, and it was these aspects which interested those studying old building traditions more and more during these years. Scholars became increasingly aware of the tremendous differences from area to area. The pioneer work of R. Mejborg in this sphere shows that he was able to demonstrate these regional variations, and his followers in the first two decades of the century, architects and others, shed considerably more light on these differences through the measuring and surveys they conducted. Moreover, they became

increasingly conscious of the fact that many of these building traditions were about to disappear.

Of great significance to Frilandsmuseet was the collaboration between Bernhard Olsen and Chr. Axel Jensen, the latter was on the staff of the National Museum but he also played a significant role in the development of more museums besides, for example the old Town Museum in Århus formed at this time. Chr. Axel Jensen's activities on behalf of the Danish Folk Museum, for instance, also included the acquisition of some old houses for the Open-Air Museum, which in turn benefited from his theoretical interest in the history of rural building traditions. He endeavoured to advance these studies by helping to prepare and send out questionnaires on old buildings, and his important work on certain types of timber construc-

The farmstead from Salling was a composite farmstead which stood on the present site of the Zealand village. The farmstead consisted of several buildings from various localities in the Salling district. The dwelling-house was from Buksager. An interesting ridge post construction was concealed behind the whitewashed walls in both the dwelling-house and outbuildings behind it.

tion *Stolper og Suler* (Posts and Ridge Posts) opened up new horizons of research.

Frilandsmuseet profited by Chr. Axel Jensen's help over the acquisition of the fisherman's hut from Nymindegab, although – as so often is the case, a local contact man was of paramount importance, in this instance a schoolteacher living in the district. There is an early record disclosing that Bernhard Olsen did not have the knack of chatting to farmers. If this is indeed correct, he had in any event a flair for allying himself with the right colleagues. It must have been necessary, too, as time passed after the opening of Frilandsmuseet in Lyngby, for he was now becoming an old man.

In the period between 1910 and c. 1915 the number of buildings at the museum increased considerably. The farmstead from North Schleswig, re-erected at this period, was an earlier plan brought to fruition by which the sequence of Bernhard Olsen's original principal categories was completed. Financial circumstances were presumably the reason why this farmstead was a composite dwelling, for in those days a complete farm of this kind could surely have been found and the piecing together thus avoided. Later in the history of Frilandsmuseet, too, this method has had to be adopted, partly due to limited funds and partly because not all old farmsteads are preserved in their entirety. In the case of the North Schleswig farmstead, the dwelling-house came from Flovt, just south of Haderslev fjord, first of all, followed later by two barns from Grønninghoved between Kolding and Haderslev, and finally a little kindling shed from Soed near Flovt. The dwelling-house was half-timbered, the greater part of which with an in-filling of bricks; at one end, however, oak boards had been used instead. The barns were solely built of oak boards between upright posts in the so-called bole-construction, earlier widespread in Denmark and a technique which survived longest in the easterly regions of North Schleswig.

This fine complex of buildings from North-East Schleswig has since had to cede its position to some houses from Zealand. The gradual enlargement of the museum's terrain that took place later, made it necessary for the earlier plans regarding the disposition of the buildings to be taken up for revision. Therefore, for a number of years all that visitors to the museum can see of the farmstead from North-East Schleswig is one of the bole-house barns from Grønninghoved standing alone.

Another farmstead acquired at about the same time has suffered a similar fate, the Salling farmstead. This building is no longer to be found in the museum park, but it is to be hoped that it will emerge from storage some day. It too would have been surrounded by buildings from Zealand if it had been allowed to remain. It was a farmstead pieced together from several, in that the dwelling-house came from Buksager in Krejbjerg parish, the barn from Krarup Møllegård, Hvidbjerg parish near Skive, and the stables and cowshed likewise from Hvidbjerg parish.

A memorable feature of this farmstead was the construction of the barn, the roof of which was supported alternately by a free-standing upright ridge post and two inclined ridge posts. Another detail, which some may perhaps remember, was a reconstruction of a stove type made of clay pots in the dwelling-room, presumably an extremely usual form of stove in the past, though no example of it has survived.

The third important acquisition made during this period is still to be found on the site allotted it. It is the skipper's cottage from Sønderho on the island of Fanø. To give the reader an idea of what the rooms would look like the museum's annual report had referred to paintings by Christen Dalsgaard, the artist, which gave an impression of the interior arrangement of farmsteads from Salling. Now in the case of the Fanø cottage it referred to the work of another genre artist Julius Exner. There is no doubt that when this cottage was re-created at the museum, the greatest emphasis was laid on its interior.

Frilandsmuseet is taken over by the State

As we have already seen, Frilandsmuseet was originally part of the Danish Folk Museum. It was also normally called "the department of buildings" or "the open-air section" of the Folk Museum, or simply "the museum of buildings". During the second decade of the present century, however, the name Frilandsmuseet became inseparably attached to just this institution, although obviously the term could be used to describe all museums of this kind.

But in spite of its name having firmly taken root by virtue of the special character and surroundings of the museum, it was formally attached to the Folk Museum and as such, part of a self-governing institution under the leadership of Bernhard Olsen, its director, assisted by a board of governors. It was not until 1920 that the Danish Folk Museum, whose collections had always been regarded as a continuation of those of the National Museum, came under the State. The Folk Museum and Frilandsmuseet together comprised a department of the National Museum until 1941 when each became separate departments.

During the years shortly before 1920 the ageing Bernhard Olsen had relinquished much of the leadership of the museum. He was most frequently to be found at the Folk Museum in Copenhagen, but he journeyed out to Frilandsmuseet once a week. A summer-house out in the museum terrain was often a meeting-place where Bernhard Olsen gave instructions to museum craftsmen and others. Ultimately he came mostly to sit on a bench in the sun outside the Ostenfeld farmstead and to enjoy the flowers. He could indeed look back on a long, successful life. In spite of opposition and criticism he had managed to guide his museums safely through many difficulties, yet no one could pursuade this authoritative old gentleman to write his memoirs for all the good material he must have had – he is supposed to have answered:"I cannot lie, but upon my word neither can I write the truth".

Jørgen Olrik took over the leadership of Frilandsmuseet in 1920 in his capacity of keeper of the Folk Museum. This outstanding, extremely learned historian and museum man, however, was a specialist in another field. He had no marked feelings for the practical side of the work at Frilandsmuseet. It is said that Bernhard Olsen was not entirely satisfied with him, remarking: "He has sat at his desk year in year out, but not an idea has he produced". It was presumably of considerable significance, under the circumstances, that when Frilandsmuseet came into the hands of the State, H. Zangenberg, architect and scholar of rural building traditions, joined the staff of the Folk Museum.

One of the advantages of becoming a state institution was an increase in security from a financial point of view. Obviously the museum had not relied solely on admission charges earlier for this is not normally possible. The Folk Museum had received government grants for many years, and when Frilandsmuseet was opened in Lyngby a number of private patrons contributed considerable donations. Funds were sometimes short, though, for the daily running of the museum, and there was no surplus to pay for research in connection with the acquisition of the old buildings; therefore a collaboration with others, for example the 2nd Department of the National Museum, was not uncommon. But in the Twenties, Zangenberg was able to begin a systematic investigation of old rural buildings in all regions of Denmark which, in turn, would provide a scholarly basis for the removal of additional farmsteads and cottages to the museum.

The problem of acquiring land on which to re-erect more buildings was also temporarily solved after Frilandsmuseet was taken over by the State. The fields adjacent to the museum bought previously by Bernhard Olsen were now purchased by the State as an undeveloped area for the enlargement of Frilandsmuseet. Others were less far-sighted. A proposal submitted by the museum for the purchase of further land adjacent to it for a modest sum because there were only very few houses on it – and which later became a residential area – never got further than the director of the National Museum. He firmly refused to pass it on to the Ministry, adding tersely (as legend would have it) "are you mad?".

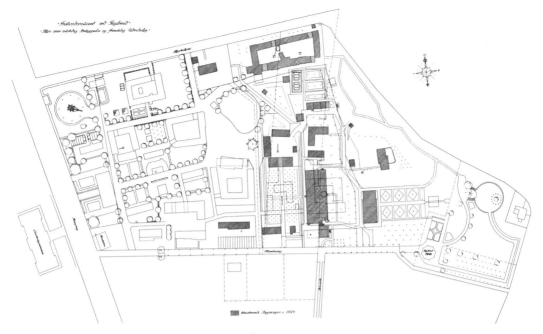

This plan drawn by Architect Zangenberg shows partly the existing buildings (dark) at Frilandsmuseet in 1924, and partly the sites planned for further buildings, as well as for the new entrance onto Kongevejen.

Frilandsmuseet 1920-1940

Although a certain measure of economic stability was provided by the State, it by no means prevented Frilandsmuseet from experiencing the cuts in national expenditure which frequently recurred in the course of the following decades. Moreover, the cautious administrators of the museum were not on the spot but in Copenhagen, in addition to which a decisive course of action was not easy to embark upon when both the Folk Museum and the director of the National Museum had to be consulted first.

A considerable amount was accomplished for Frilandsmuseet by Architect Zangenberg during the Twenties and Thirties. His groundplans and photographs of old rural buildings are numerous, but he was rarely photographed himself. He sits here by the splashmill from Småland in 1924. This was the first building Zangenberg removed to the museum.

33

Nevertheless, through the regional surveys undertaken by the Folk Museum and Frilandsmuseet, not only were significant old buildings located – a number of them were also bought and moved to Lyngby. The first to be erected after the reorganisation of the museum was again a building from Sweden, namely a little water mill (a "splash" mill) with horizontal wheel from Småland. This was soon followed by a post mill from Karlstrup near Køge in Zealand, and as it stands close to the busy main road Kongevejen it soon became a kind of trademark for the museum.

The nucleus representing different types of old mills was thus formed at Frilandsmuseet. A later form of windmill, the Dutch type in which only the cap carrying the sails was turned to the wind, had long been in the vicinity although not owned by the museum. It was the fine Fuglevad windmill situated just outside

the boundary. It had been allowed to fall into disrepair for some years and the intention was to demolish it. Fortunately, it was purchased by a private citizen in 1917 and saved from destruction. He arranged for it to be restored and donated it to the Agricultural Museum; however, it was not formally part of Frilandsmuseet until 1937.

When the middle of the Thirties was reached it was fairly easy to perceive that an effort had been made over a number of years to move buildings from various regions of Denmark to the museum. The geographical criteria concerning the selection of buildings had clearly had an effect, but there were still many gaps. Moreover, many old buildings simply had to be sa-

On Midsummer Day 1926 the 25th anniversary was celebrated of the opening of Frilandsmuseet at Sorgenfri in 1901. On the slope below the Fuglevad windmill wellwishers listened to speeches and watched folk dancing. Seated on a bench in the middle is the Danish poet Jeppe Aakjær. On a bench in front of him is the Permanent Secretary at the Ministry of Education. Nearest the dancers is the folklore scholar H. Ellekilde.

ved without delay for they were fast disappearing, and this meant that now and again buildings were brought to the museum which could not be re-erected at once. They were at least safe and could be put up again when funds permitted.

Of the buildings re-erected and opened to the public at this period can be mentioned the fisherman's cottage from Agger, North-West Jutland, the farmstead from Lundager in Funen, and also from the same island, the smallholder's farmstead from Årup, as well as the forge from Ørbæk. A major part of the museum's activities, however, was not immediately evident to visitors; this was the work involved with the buildings which were opened to the public during the period that followed. Indeed, some of the buildings acquired at that time have not yet unfortunately been re-erected. This applies, for example, to the farmstead from Elling, northern Jutland, and from Zealand the cottage from Hornbæk and the farmstead from Gevinge. The latter was exhibited for a short time at a large agricultural show at Bellahøj, on the outskirts of Copenhagen, in 1938 to commemorate the 150th anniversary of the abolition of adscription. The church stable from Bregninge on the island of Ærø was re-erected at the museum for some years but has since been taken down again.

It was to H. Zangenberg's unfailing credit that during these years, at the same time as organising the practical side of running Frilandsmuseet and its gradual

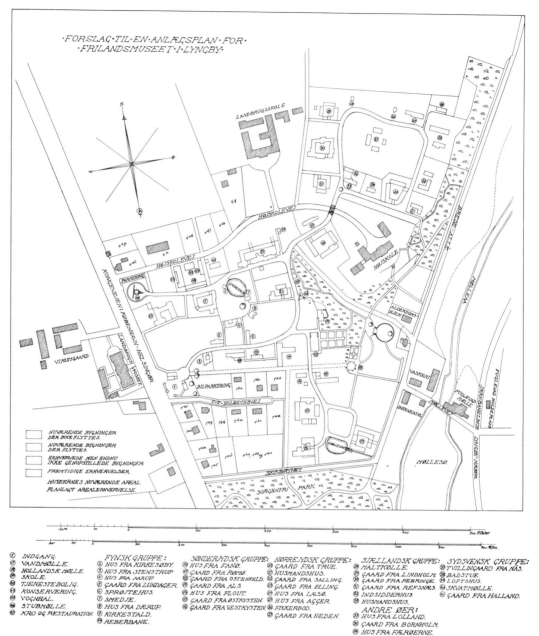

·FORSLAG·TIL·EN·ANLÆGSPLAN·FOR·
·FRILANDSMUSEET·I·LYNGBY·

NUVÆRENDE BYGNINGER
DER IKKE FLYTTES.
NUVÆRENDE BYGNINGER
DER FLYTTES.
ERHVERVEDE MEN ENDNU
IKKE GENOPSTILLEDE BYGNINGER.
FREMTIDIGE ERHVERVELSER.

MUSEERNES NUVÆRENDE AREAL.
PLANLAGT AREALERHVERVELSE.

① INDGANG.
② VANDMØLLE.
③ HOLLANDSK MØLLE.
④ SKOLE.
⑤ TJENESTEBOLIG.
⑥ KONSERVERING.
⑦ VOGNHAL.
⑧ STUBMØLLE.
⑨ KRO OG RESTAURATION.

FYNSK GRUPPE:
② HUS FRA KIRKESØBY.
③ HUS FRA STENSTRUP.
④ HUS FRA AARUP.
⑤ GAARD FRA LUNDAGER.
⑥ SPRØJTEHUS.
⑦ SMEDJE.
⑧ HUS FRA DÆRUP.
⑨ KIRKESTALD.
⑩ REBERBANE.

SØNDERJYDSK GRUPPE:
⑯ HUS FRA FANØ.
⑰ GAARD FRA RØMØ.
⑱ GAARD FRA OSTENFELD.
⑲ GAARD FRA ALS.
⑳ HUS FRA FLOUT.
㉑ GAARD FRA ØSTKYSTEN.
㉒ GAARD FRA VESTKYSTEN.

NØRREJYDSK GRUPPE:
㉓ GAARD FRA TRUE.
㉔ HUSMANDSHUS.
㉕ GAARD FRA SALLING.
㉖ GAARD FRA ELLING.
㉗ HUS FRA LÆSØ.
㉘ HUS FRA AGGER.
㉙ FISKERBOD.
㉚ GAARD FRA HEDEN.

SJÆLLANDSK GRUPPE:
㉛ MALTKØLLE.
㉜ GAARD FRA LINDHOLM.
㉝ GAARD FRA PEBRINGE.
㉞ GAARD FRA REFSNÆS.
㉟ INDSIDDERHUS.
㊱ HUSMANDSHUS.
ANDRE ØER:
㊲ HUS FRA LOLLAND.
㊳ GAARD FRA BORNHOLM.
㊴ HUS FRA FÆRØERNE.

SYDSVENSK GRUPPE:
㊵ TVILLINGAARD FRA NÄS.
㊶ BADSTUE.
㊷ LOFTSHUS.
㊸ SKVATMØLLE.
㊹ GAARD FRA HALLAND.

This proposal for the development of Frilandsmuseet was prepared by Architect Zangenberg in 1930. The idea had begun to take shape of extending the museum park to the north of the folk high-school. The plan was originally intended to be set out in colour which explains why the key has not been used.

Already by 1935 there were parking problems at Frilandsmuseet. Cars had to park on each side of the main road. The white house was the premises of Kafé Fuglevad. It was succeeded by Frilandsmuseet's Restaurant in one of the wings of the new entrance building completed two years later.

expansion, he also gathered an enormous amount of material about the rural building traditions of the entire country. His surveys and measurements, sketch groundplans and descriptions mounted steadily in the archives of the Folk Museum, and article after article on the building customs of various regions flowed from his pen. Frilandsmuseet was not particularly big at that time, it is true, and the burden of running it not particularly heavy, and he was clearly unable to take part personally in every detail. Occasionally a building was dismantled in the countryside which he did not supervise, and if this was the case the museum custodian Mr. Teglbjærg attended to it.

Gradually, though, Zangenberg received help with both investigations in the field and the removal of buildings to the museum. Arne Ludvigsen, the architect, was a very considerable help in the work of recording the rural building traditions of Funen, and from the latter half of the Thirties he also took part in the removal of buildings. In this he made a notable contribution to the development of the techniques for moving old buildings. The first building for Frilandsmuseet to be moved by him was the smallholder's farmstead from Kirke-Søby in Funen. This was re-erected beside the farmstead from Årup which Zangenberg had moved. Therefore, it is possible to compare the results of the two different methods of removal.

The Årup farmstead, for example, like

37

The clogmaker's cottage in the process of being dismantled in its native village of Kirke-Søby on Funen. The exterior of the bread oven is well preserved. The outside wall has been taken down and it is possible to follow the graduated profile of the bread oven as far as the scullery chimney. The cottage was dismantled in 1937.

the Lundager farmstead and the other buildings moved to the museum early on, appears perhaps a little hard and angular in its lines. This is due to the fact that Zangenberg eliminated the dilapidations which often marked the old buildings acquired by the museum. He did not intend to exhibit the buildings as they had been handed down to us in the course of time, but rather as the peasants would have wished them to appear when they were built. Arne Ludvigsen, on the other hand, wanted to show the buildings with their signs of earlier habitation. While Zangenberg changed out dilapidated timber and righted irregularities, Ludvigsen was of the opinion that it gave life to buildings if these traces of wear and tear were allowed to remain.

The latter method could lead to a somewhat haphazard re-creation of fortuitous details in an advanced state of disrepair when carried to extremes. Its culminating point was reached with the re-erection of the farmstead from Pebringe in Zealand; although it was not completed until the period that followed, it was taken down in the late Thirties. At the same time, work was in progress on the re-erection of the farmstead from Rømø – perhaps the most successful removal undertaken by Ludvigsen. The scrupulous re-creation of the brickwork of this farmstead illustrates how the mellowness of an old brick building can be maintained after a move, in comparison say to one of the buildings mentioned earlier – the cottage from Fanø.

The re-erection of the Rømø farmstead was completed in 1940 on a newly acquired piece of land north of the original museum terrain. The new acreage provided the open spaces needed to convey to the visitor that the old building had originally been in an isolated position with no other houses close to it. Moreover, there was now space enough to start thinking about the landscaping of the surroundings in which the buildings were situated. The northerly tract of land now purchased, became the first expanse of heath in Frilandsmuseet.

This expansion in 1940 depended particularly on two factors, and had been under preparation for a number of years. Firstly, the folk high-school had decided to move, and secondly the financial position of Frilandsmuseet had improved in connection with the rebuilding of the National Museum's premises in Prinsens Palæ in the Thirties. A law passed in 1933 concerning the National Museum and Folk Museum stipulated that the Folk Museum and Frilandsmuseet were not after all to be situated adjacent to each other. And in order not to abandon Frilandsmuseet entirely, a number of special

When the Rømø farmstead was completed in 1940 the fact that a brick building could be so successfully moved caused a sensation. The open chimney in the kitchen is a good example of how old brickwork can be sensitively re-created, and the aesthetic value of such details is considerable. The farmstead represents a fine, well arranged 18th century home. But the open chimney tells us about a way of life very different to that of today – especially for the housewife.

government grants were made to the museum. It was these funds which enabled the purchase of the buildings and grounds of the high-school, as well as a little of the land owned by the Agricultural College and a couple of houses along the Kongevej.

What had earlier been the high-school buildings were now used by the museum as workshops etc. It bacame a small enclave in the museum park which visitors still have to avoid by a detour to this day. A new entrance building facing Kongevejen (partly where the houses had been) was finished in 1937, the architect was Mogens Clemmensen. The three-winged building had a restaurant in the southerly half. This followed tradition, for one of the demolished houses had had a little café on the premises. The Frilandsmuseet Restaurant was destined to enjoy a considerable reputation, not least during its first years under the name Hammers Kro. The northerly half of the entrance building was used for storing wagons. It was not until much later – in 1970 – that the present entrance hall and other public facilities were arranged. Earlier, visitors were served from a ticket office in a whistling draught in the gateway. The pair of lions was moved to the new entrance, where they still stand overlooking the main road. The small road Museumsvej was closed and the wooden buildings comprising the earlier entrance removed shortly afterwards.

Frilandsmuseet 1940-1960

As from 1940, the old sunken road cutting through the slopes to Mølleåen was no longer the museum boundary. The expansion meant that the museum totalled c. 40 acres. Frilandsmuseet was growing into a big museum after many years as a comparatively small one. The mixture of highly heterogeneous buildings situated close together, the relics of a vanished past, was indeed striking. For many years it had been a garden – a little overgrown and confusing to the eye in a curious bewitched slumber.

A new form of planning was now essential. A general plan had always been followed for the expansion of Frilandsmuseet. The purpose of the collection had to be kept clearly in mind to ensure that the right buildings were selected and set in the right surroundings in the museum park. We have heard about Bernhard Olsen's evolutionary sequence which was the first principle of collection when the museum was started. The later aim of finding buildings to represent the building traditions of various parts of the country has also been mentioned. The next stage, then, was the gradual realisation that the museum should also show the social strata in which the rural population had been divided.

The increased area at the disposal of Frilandsmuseet meant that the plans for expansion could be revised for it provided the opportunity of grouping buildings according to region. Buildings from Jutland could be moved out to the north zone

Some of the outer walls of the Pebringe farmstead are so crooked it is remarkable that they remain standing. The farmstead was re-erected with all the wear and tear, dilapidations and irregularities acquired in the course of generations. Visitors to the museum can in many ways follow the constant struggle of past occupants to keep the buildings in repair.

where it was possible to re-create their settings as single farmsteads isolated in the landscape. A village from East Jutland could spring up at the edge of the newly acquired terrain, and buildings from Funen and Zealand would have enough room to convey a village setting in the original part of the museum. The buildings from Funen had already in the Thirties the character of a village, with a village pond in the middle edged with pollarded poplars. From the village meeting place – a ring of stones under a lime tree – one can glance over to the homes of the villagers: the farmer, the smallholder, the clogmaker and the blacksmith. Here were the social divisions that had become part of the principles of selection, and here, too, the landscaping of the buildings' original setting which was to

become even more convincing as more land was acquired.

Shortly after the purchase of the new land, various changes took place in the administration of the museum, for both Olrik and Zangenberg died. A move that had become increasingly necessary: the separation of Frilandsmuseet and the Folk Museum was carried out. Frilandsmuseet had become so large, and the countless practical problems to be solved daily so foreign to the work of a normal museum, that an administrative separation was the only feasible solution.

In 1941, therefore, Frilandsmuseet became an independent department of the National Museum. Its leader was Kai Uldall, who had been attached to the Folk Museum for many years. He was originally on the staff of the Medieval

This plan shows proposals for the development of Frilands-museet during the latter part of the Forties and early Fifties. All completed re-erections are marked in black. The plan was prepared and drawn by Arne Ludvigsen and Frode Kirk in 1950. At that period an even distribution of buildings was expected throughout the entire area the museum hoped to acquire. A site was set aside for a sugar mill from a former Danish possession in the West Indies, as well as for reconstructions of prehistoric dwellings.

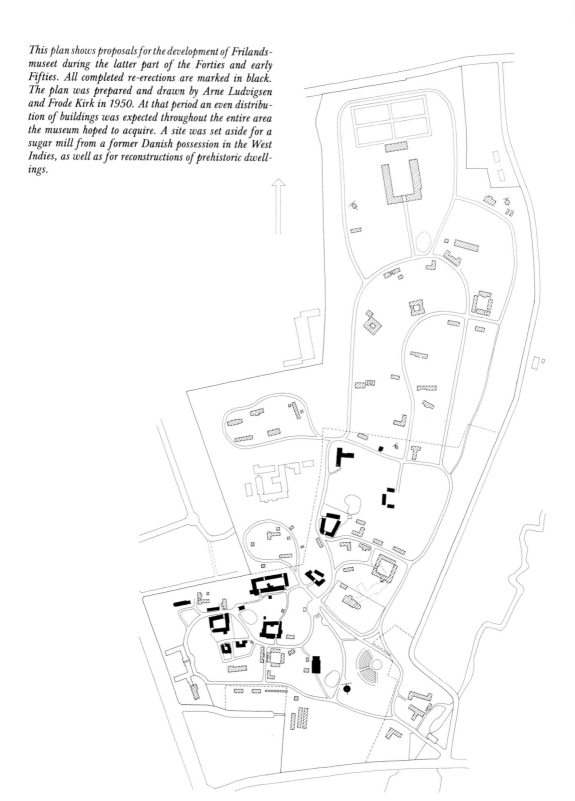

Department of the National Museum, and had long been deeply engaged with the work of both museums. From the second half of the Twenties he had also had a certain amount to do with Frilandsmuseet, particularly the acquisition of items for its collections during his journeys in the countryside. During the latter part of the Thirties, however, Kai Uldall participated more and more directly in the work of Frilandsmuseet, and his appointment as its leader was a natural choice. It was indeed a happy solution for the museum which now had an independent administration on the spot. Uldall remained the leader of the museum until he reached the age of retirement in 1960.

The fact that Frilandsmuseet had become a state owned institution in no way prevented private benefactors from giving their support. Several of the most important acquisitions were in reality due to extremely generous donations given privately. For example, the farmstead from Ostenfeld was moved to the museum as a result of a donation from Mr. Serdin Hansen, the merchant, and the farmstead from Rømø was likewise transferred with the financial support of Mr. A.P. Møller, the ship-owner. A society called *Frilandsmuseets Venner* (The Friends of Frilandsmuseet) was formed in 1940 in order to administer all private donations, both large and small, in the best possible way. Mr. V. Falbe-Hansen, the barrister, played a major role in this respect. He was chairman of the committee for the society for the next twenty-eight years, and during the last years of his life the society's honorary member.

The economy of Frilandsmuseet is naturally based on the annual grants under the Finance Bill passed in parliament like any other state institution. When the budget for the museum is drawn up every effort is made to cover the expenses by running it in the most effective way, but

Kai Uldall photographed in 1960, the year he retired from Frilandsmuseet.

there is something called budget cuts, and these have sometimes hit the museum rather badly. Sometimes, too, the museum suddenly has the opportunity of making an important acquisition which could not be foreseen when the budget was made. Therefore, the private financial aid provided by *Frilandsmuseets Venner* is of invaluable help to the museum.

It was also important for the museum to have funds available for another form of transaction which could be negotiated without delay if the need arose, namely extensions to the museum park. The purchase of large areas would normally be negotiated at length and in exhaustive detail. However, if a small neighbouring property protruding into the museum's land suddenly came up for sale, it would always be expedient to be able to purchase without hesitation. This was the

aim of *Frilandsmuseets Grundkøbsfond* established in 1945 with the support of the Lyngby-Tårbæk borough council, in whose district the museum lies. It has since enabled various purchases to be made for a minor rounding off of the museum park, but has otherwise suffered from an almost chronic shortage of money.

Upon the death of H. Zangenberg, the post of museum architect passed to Arne Ludvigsen, who remained with the museum until 1951. The task fell to him to re-erect a number of the buildings which had been acquired by the museum in the foregoing period. It was now possible to group the buildings according to region. In the north zone, for example, the farmstead from Kølvrå on Karup Heath was re-erected in a solitary position, separated from the Rømø farmstead by the newly landscaped belt of heathland. The four-winged steading from True near Århus, a large red-washed farm, was the beginning of the East Jutland village.

The large white farmstead from Pebringe in Zealand is the clearest example of the principles for the removal of old buildings upheld by Arne Ludvigsen. Here, all the irregularities, all the strange small innovations and repairs of successive generations of farmers are faithfully preserved. This farmstead is first and foremost a stirring monument to the tenacity of the Danish peasantry, for it is not only the buildings which tell us of the additions and alterations made in the course of centuries. When an old building is moved, the site on which it stood is excavated, and these excavations reveal the traces of far earlier habitations on the same spot.

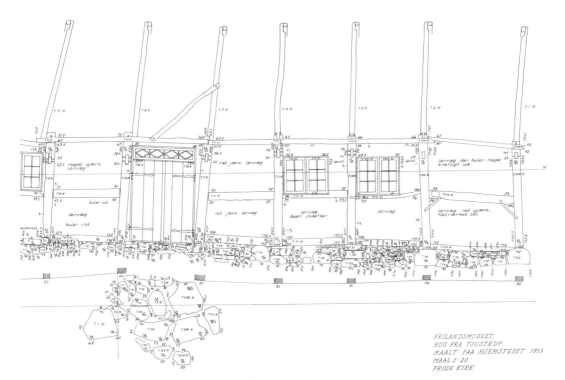

FRILANDSMUSEET.
HUS FRA TJUSTRUP.
MAALT PAA HJEMSTEDET 1953
MAAL 1 :20
FRODE KIRK

Elevation of the weaver's cottage from Tystrup in Zealand. The measurements were taken in preparation for its removal to the museum in 1953. The numbers are partly notes of measurement and partly numbered structural details.

The archeological investigation of these plots was first undertaken in about 1940. The site of the Lundager farmstead, for example, was excavated but here no earlier traces of habitation were found.

By and large the moving of buildings during the Fifties followed the same lines as during the preceding years. The measuring and surveying techniques were the same, although the criteria as to how the buildings were to be re-erected underwent some modification. It was no longer considered desirable to re-create all the anomalies of an old building after its removal to the museum. Very often the structure of a building had suffered severely from neglect during its latter years in situ, and it often fell to the museum to take over buildings which had not been kept in repair for some time, or which were even

uninhabited and derelict. Better maintained farmsteads and cottages, on the other hand, were usually so modernised that they were unsuited for removal; in addition to which a building of this sort was too expensive to buy.

A glance at some of the buildings re-erected during the Fifties, however, reveals clearly the moderation of conservation principles. After the early, extremely heavy restorations, and the later sensitive re-creation of precisely what was found, a happy medium had now been reached. Buildings opened to the public at this time were for example, the weaver's cottage from Tystrup in Zealand, the smallholder's farmstead from Dannemare in Lolland and the farmstead from the island of Læsø in the Kattegat.

However, although the earlier programme laid down for the expansion of the museum was thus being followed, it was once again taken up for revision. This was

45

The conservation of the landscape in the museum park is part of the long-term planning for Frilandsmuseet. For example, the ancient stand of oak on the slopes down to the river Mølleå is carefully tended. This includes felling a later growth of beech and sycamore which threatens to suffocate the oak trees. The tree falling to the ground here was felled to give the oaks more light. Young oaks are planted in the clearings.

due to the fact that a new opportunity for extending the museum park arose. When the first plot of land was purchased and the museum moved to Lyngby, its situation beside two colleges of adult education influenced the choice but never played a great role, though all the pupils from both institutions undoubtedly visited the old farmsteads and cottages in the museum. The great stroke of good fortune for the museum was that both colleges had considerable grounds adjoining the museum park, which remained undeveloped at a period when the surrounding district rapidly became a built-up suburb of Copenhagen. The Lyngby Agricultural College was now about to follow in the footsteps of the high-school in the Thirties. Plans were made to move the college away from town to the countryside.

Frilandsmuseet swiftly produced, in its turn, plans to show how an extension to the north over the land now available would provide the opportunity for creating an ideal museum of its kind.

To begin with, there was much optimism about how the additional space could be used if the museum were extended north as far as Brede. But a more realistic view began to take shape when it was realised that there would still only be enough space for the types of building already scheduled for re-erection. If the landscaping principles were to be maintained an essential prerequisite was sufficient land. Therefore, the somewhat romantic thought of moving houses from Greenland and the former Danish West Indies to the museum was abandoned, although the idea of reconstructing prehistoric dwellings proved more long-lived.

It was crucial to the development of Frilandsmuseet and its position as one of the leading museums of its kind that these plans for expansion bore fruit. In two instalments, in 1953 and 1957, the area north of the old boundary as fas as and including Brede home farm was purchased, together with the Agricultural College and its land. The college buildings became workshops, storerooms and offices, and the old stables the winter quarters for livestock belonging to the museum.

The large area acquired by Frilandsmuseet was opened to the public in 1960, and at the same time the first building in the new terrain: the large, strange marshland farmstead from Eiderstedt,

South Schleswig. This memorable double event was Kai Uldall's farewell upon entering into retirement. It can safely be said that Bernhard Olsen founded Frilandsmuseet, but the fact that it became a large museum is without doubt due above all to the insight of Kai Uldall. For his ability to make the museum known and well-loved among an enormous number of people, contributed conclusively to the positive attitude of the authorities, whose financial support was so essential to the development of the museum. And Frilandsmuseet, moreover, has reaped the benefit for many years of Kai Uldall's deep knowledge of all aspects of Danish folk culture.

Frilandsmuseet after 1960

When the old north boundary fence was removed in 1960, and the public could move into the new northerly area of the museum park, it meant that the museum was more than twice as large as hitherto. A minor rounding off of the park has also taken place by degrees after this – Frilandsmuseet has now grown from c. 6 acres in 1901 to approximately 90 acres today.

The additional acreage made it possible for greatly improved planning to be brought into effect when more buildings were gradually re-erected. The sequence of building was altered, in order to begin building on the large newly acquired tract of land without undue delay. The farmstead from Eiderstedt stood here in splendid isolation, but in the long run perhaps its situation was too dominant. A number of years, however, was destined to pass before the re-erection of further buildings in this area could be completed. In the meantime, a watermill from Funen was under construction which gave rise to

complicated technical arrangements. The mill pond was excavated behind a large dam, and the water for the pond was borrowed from the river Mølleåen. Water pumped into it from the river, though, was not used solely by the watermill, for a certain amount passed further into the museum to the village pond by the forge, and to the splashmill from Småland. And likewise, it was also water from Mølleåen that later maintained the water level in the dykes round the Eiderstedt farmstead, and which by means of an artificial Jutland stream led out to a "fire" pond in the extreme northern end of the museum, and then further to the splashmill from the Faroe Islands.

Work soon began on the erection of buildings in the newly-opened terrain. These buildings came from regions where there was often a considerable distance between farmsteads, and the intention to give them the same setting in the museum could be carried out, as can be seen from the position, for example, of the farmsteads from Vemb and Lønnestak in West Jutland. A complete farmstead from the

The beer room by the kitchen in the watermill from Funen gives some impression of rural housekeeping in the old days. Food was prepared and preserved in quantity to ensure a lasting supply of provisions for long periods at a time. The beer barrels bear witness of home brewing, a custom which survived longest on Funen. Preserving jars are ranged along shelves covered with newspaper cut in scallops.

Faroes was re-erected on the slopes of the Mølleå river valley instead of the old imitation Faroese house. The little settlement is intended to be seen from the lower slopes with blinkers on as it were. In this way, it is possible to eliminate the local North Zealand landscape, and experience simply the steep grassy slopes – for all the world like a little piece of the Faroe Islands. Buildings have also been added to the earlier part of the museum in the past few years. The cottage from Ødis Bramdrup supplements the East Jutland village already begun. The smallholder's cottage from Dörröd illustrates the building traditions of south-west Scania which so resemble those of Zealand, and moreover a very necessary addition to the museum in order to prevent visitors from being misled by the strangeness of the

Näsgård farmsteads. The North Schleswig (or South Jutland) element has also been strengthened by the erection of one of the largest farmsteads in the museum – from Sønder Sejerslev, and from the same parish: the little cottage from Nørre Sejerslev.

The two last-mentioned buildings are a good example of the importance attached to the task of showing the social divisions in the rural population. For here, from virtually the same spot is the modest cottage beside the prosperous farmstead. Earlier criteria for the selection of buildings are still applied, for example it is still the aim to have the major regional types of rural building represented, but there are a number of serious deficiencies in this respect which must be corrected. The question of period is clearly based on

48

the criterium that a conscious effort must be made to represent different periods.

The tendency in recent years has been to choose slightly later stages in the history of a building when arranging the interiors, than was perhaps formerly the case. For example, the arrangement of the interior of the watermill from Funen was originally to be rather old-fashioned to correspond with the age of the building. However, when the time came to re-erect it after a number of years in store, the point of view had changed. The decision was made to arrange the interior as it had been during the lifetime of the last miller and his wife. Some of the old furniture acquired for the watermill was therefore put in the loft as more or less obsolete items. While the furniture in the building when acquired by the museum was now brought out. In addition to which, a daughter of the last miller helped the museum to re-create this milieu from the close of the 19th century. She had cherished her old home, and it was hard for her to leave when the building was about to be dismantled. Thus, at the age of 85 she was able to come to the museum and tell us where all the small ornaments should be.

The old miller's daughter could also describe the lay-out of the garden, and what flowers it had. As with all removals to the museum, the immediate vicinity of the building was surveyed and measured, and a plan of the garden made on which the plants, bushes etc. in it were recorded. In order to be absolutely sure that the right species were planted when the old garden was re-created at the museum,

49

The dismantling and transport of the buildings from the Faroe Islands in 1961 was undertaken under somewhat difficult conditions. For example, the surface of the panelling removed from the living-room should on no account get wet – not easy to manage in a rainy climate like the Faroes. In the village of Múla a ropeway had to be made for conveying every plank and stone over the edge of the cliff down to the boat.

plants and seeds were collected from it – as is always done – and graft cuttings taken from its fruit trees.

Great care is constantly taken over the setting of every building, therefore it can be said that the interior principle applied to the inside of a building has been developed to apply to its exterior. But this obviously necessitates sufficient space, and it was not until 1940 with the enlargement of the museum park, that these ideas could be carried out in practice and evolved still further.

Apart from the gardens of farmsteads, an effort is made to re-create the native vegetation of a region, we have already mentioned heathland for example. A lot is being done to preserve the woods in the museum. By a stroke of good fortune, when the area sloping down to the Mølleå

was taken over by the museum, it included an ancient oak-wood which is, in itself, an interesting piece of forestry history. Moreover, a little of the uses of a wood in former times is revealed, when a visitor to the museum comes across an old royal game preserve stone at the corner of a woodland path. Scattered round the museum park, then, are some of the relics that may still be encountered in the countryside. For example, the first milestone was already put up in the Twenties and more have followed since. The stream that now winds past the farmstead from Vemb can be crossed by a splendid old granite bridge from the same region.

The landscape in Frilandsmuseet is very much part of what the museum wants to show its visitors. A walk through the terrain gives more than a hint of the habi-

tation patterns of bygone days in Denmark, and of the history of the rural landscape. It is an important part of what is characteristic for Frilandsmuseet. It is not simply a frame about the main contents of the museum, but a reason why the aim of the museum can be more far-reaching than a normal museum. As apart from having the usual cultural purpose of institutions of this kind, Frilandsmuseet has very considerable recreative qualities.

The work of museums is sometimes divided into three categories: collection and preservation, research, and enlightenment. The first category is obviously of primary importance, because without it there would be nothing to work with in respect of the next two categories. Research is invaluable, for without it no lines could be laid down for satisfactory principles of collection, just as information about the collected exhibits cannot be properly imparted if there is no underlying research to support it. Enlightenment may be equated with the process of imparting the work of a museum to a wider public – to be informative and a source of pleasure to as many people as possible.

This process of communication is many things. First and foremost, quite simply the fact that the museum is open and people can walk round and see what is in it. Then there are the illustrated guides that can be bought which explain the contents of the museum, and if more detailed information about a building is desired there are other publications to turn to. These can be purchased in the entrance hall arranged a few years ago in the yellow buildings of the main entrance on Konge-

vejen. For those who would rather listen than read there are numerous guided tours round the museum. In 1963 Frilandsmuseet established a special educational department for the purpose of helping schoolchildren and also students, as well as preparing courses for schoolteachers on how the contents of the museum can be exploited for teaching purposes. There is, moreover, an old tradition whereby demonstration models of some of the tools and implements in the various cottages and farmsteads are used to show the different kinds of handicrafts for which the originals were used, and which have since died out. Candle-making and pottery-making are demonstrated during the summer months. Lace-making, spinning and weaving are also shown, there is sometimes an opportunity to see where the wool comes from when it is shearing time for the museum's sheep.

There has been livestock at the museum for a long time, but in the course of the Sixties the number has considerably increased primarily because of the expansion of the museum. Yet there are limits to how many animals can be kept as pastureland decreases each time a building is re-erected. The experience of watching the various species of livestock in rural surroundings in many ways enlightens city children, but it is not only them by any means. Sometimes children who have been bred and brought up in the country experience their first drive in a horse-drawn wagon at Frilandsmuseet.

The entrance building completed in 1937 was intended for a smaller public than that visiting the museum 30-40 years later. Now visitors enter the museum through this new main hall after the modernisation in 1970, and postcards and publications about Frilandsmuseet may be chosen in comfort.

Farm animals and wagons are borderline cases between the educational and the recreative. Livestock tells us about the various kinds of animal husbandry and its significance under changing geographical conditions. It is not a coincidence that the cattle grazing round the marshland Eiderstedt farmstead are the black and white Frisian variety. The horse-drawn wagon also has a serious function, as it helps those who have difficulty in walking round the museum park on foot, for the distance to the most outlying farmsteads is now considerable after the new land has been brought into use. Obviously, though, the presence of grazing animals

and horse-drawn wagons primarily give life and local colour to their surroundings.

One of the aims of the museum is to encourage its visitors to absorb what they see in a relaxed and undemanding fashion, combining the educational side of a museum visit with a pleasant outing or walk. One of the museum's great assets is the miscellany of walks that can be decided upon, both long and short, according to taste. One can choose whether to look round a general selection of buildings, or whether to concentrate on buildings from a certain part of the country, or for example craftsmen's cottages or mills. Or one can just decide to go for a walk through an ever-changing landscape, free from noisy traffic and urban conditions.

The spirit of an outing can be enhanced by the knowledge that it is possible to eat a picnic lunch if one needs a rest during

A folk dancing festival was held at Frilandsmuseet on 6th July 1969. Many teams of dancers gave displays in the arena and round about between the houses. 7000 people visited the museum that day – a record which is not yet broken, and crowds watched the dancing in the arena.

or after the tour. There are a number of picnic places for this purpose scattered round about the museum. They are arranged like refreshment places in the old days with fixed wooden tables and benches, and in the central clearing is also a kiosk where light refreshments are to be bought. The former restaurant in the entrance building has now been converted to a cafeteria.

A special form of entertainment is also provided by folk dancing displays which, apart from being entertaining, reveal something about life in the past. The colourful costumes of the folk dancers show how the countryfolk in different parts of the country dressed for festive occasions. But again it is above all entertaining for visitors of all ages to sit and enjoy folk dancing in full swing on a Saturday or Sunday afternoon. The museum owes a debt of gratitude in this respect to the many folk dance societies without whose help these displays could not be arranged summer after summer. Occasionally a troupe from abroad pays a visit and adds zest with a glimpse of foreign temperament in the dancing.

It was at the time of the 25th anniversary of Frilandsmuseet in 1926 that folk dancing was introduced to the museum, and since then the number of displays has increased year by year until during the Sixties every Saturday and Sunday

The little yellow summer-house used temporarily as a ticket office at the museum's north entrance since 1965. One day, when this entrance is rearranged, the summer-house will stand in a manor-house garden. In the past many large gardens and parks contained one or more small buildings of this kind. The summer-house shown here comes from a garden in Stege overlooking Stege Nor on the island of Møn. It dates from c. 1800.

throughout the summer was booked. For many years the displays were given where the garden of the watermill from Funen now is, the audience simply sat on the grassy slopes. In 1965, however, the amphitheatrelike open-air dancing green was completed in the northern end of the museum.

The folk dancing and other recreative aspects of Frilandsmuseet have naturally attracted many visitors to the museum, although only a relatively small percentage attended the folk dancing displays, *viz.* about 10% in 1972. Arrangements of this kind, however, and the general green-belt quality of the museum park encourage people to visit the museum who are not otherwise particularly interested in museums. A good deal no doubt becomes more interested when casually visiting an old building on the way to or from the dancing green. Otherwise it is indisputably the combination of landscape and museum which has strongly contributed towards the popularity of the museum among the general public. In any event, Frilandsmuseet has gradually become one of the most frequented museums in Denmark, visited annually by more than 180.000 people.

The high visiting figures necessitated a gradual extension of the facilities available to the public. For example, the extra entrance at the northerly end of the park on the way down to Brede with a large car park to supplement that by the southerly entrance. This car park is now also used by visitors to the National Museum's exhibitions in some of Brede's old factory buildings, which have been taken over for museum use by the State. The temporary ticket office at the new north entrance was installed in a summer-house from a garden in Stege on the island of Møn.

Frilandsmuseet in coming years

The reason why the north entrance is to be altered in time lies in the plans of putting up a manor house on the site. Part of the area here as well as the summer-house are to be incorporated in the gardens of the coming manor house, and one of the farm buildings attached to it is already on the site: the large half-timbered barn, for this was the building the peasants knew best. Here they had to work at the most wearing task of villeinage before the land reforms: threshing.

With the manor house the highest social layer of the rural population will be represented, and it is a need which the museum must fulfil in the years to come. But some future tasks are more pressing, for example a somewhat better representation of the living conditions among the lowest social groups of the rural population. The landless – one could perhaps say those almost entirely without possessions, leave little to posterity. It is even difficult from a technical point of view to re-create their living conditions, typified for the most part by damp, dirt, smells and a random collection of junk.

One of the best possibilities of retaining a relic of the social misery of former times would presumably be to move a workhouse to the museum. The arrangement of the interior will present difficulties. Other communal buildings ought to be acquired as well – the church and village school. Both the manor house and church have a common element which works to the advantage of the museum: time. For they are among the buildings whose original function will be increasingly difficult to maintain, but which are nevertheless comparatively well kept. On the other hand, the museum will have to act quickly on other fronts.

Gaps still exist, moreover, in the regional representation of buildings at the museum. Some buildings have been taken to the museum and stored here, it is true, for a number of years, but others have not yet been acquired. Some of the weaknesses of the museum spring quickly to the eye during a walk through it. Bornholm is solely represented by a very little mill. The intention is to erect a complete farmstead on the slopes above it from this island. The museum should also have a building from North Zealand, in which can be seen the special technique of half-timbering in this area. North Jutland is not well represented on the map showing the native localities of the museum's buildings.

It is very evident, then, that Frilandsmuseet has enough work to embark upon in the coming years. The general plan for the expansion of the collection of buildings has obviously had to be revised from time to time and brought up to date. It has still not yet been fully implemented, though, even after pursuing a consistent policy for a number of years. As mentioned earlier, some buildings are still missing from the viewpoint of both social and regional criteria for a completely balanced representation of early Danish folk culture.

The period within which the museum operates also needs to be taken up for revision.

In practice, no buildings later than the mid-1800's have been moved to the museum; on the other hand, the latest interior arrangements are from the close of the century even though they are to be found in buildings which are somewhat older. Some of these later interiors, for example in the cottage from Englerup, in the watermill from Funen, and in the

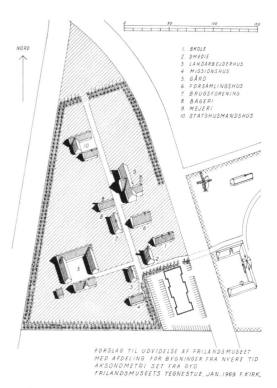

This is the first proposal for siting the buildings of the co-operative era in the new department of Frilandsmuseet. Several variations of this proposal have since been prepared.

farmstead from Sønder Sejerslev, appear to appeal to the public to quite a striking degree. This may possibly be explained by the fact that they are not totally unfamiliar. In some of the rooms people recognise the Victorian furniture and ornaments they have otherwise associated with the times of their grandparents.

It is important for Frilandsmuseet to serve its public by acting as a link between the past and present. The old buildings at the museum then appeal more to the modern public. And, moreover, the earliest phase of our industrial society is now so distant that the memory of the conditions which prevailed then is fading. It is therefore very natural that Frilandsmuseet should endeavour to keep pace, and with this in mind, plans have been made for opening a new department to span the period from c. 1880 to c. 1950.

The new department will be situated on the other side of Kongevejen, bounded by the Lyngby bypass to the west. The buildings will include a farmstead, a State smallholding, a farm labourer's cottage, as well as a village school, village hall, chapel, a forge and machine shop, a bakery, a co-operative store and a co-operative dairy. These buildings will portray an epoch marked not only by the co-operative movement, but also by the ever-growing interaction between agriculture and industry, not to mention increasing mechanisation. The dwindling number of people engaged in farming is characteristic of this period as a whole – the striking differences of the old peasant culture from region to region have blurred, increasing uniformity has obliterated many of the former differences between urban and rural society, the furnishing and arrangement of the home, for example.

Although the buildings of the recent period will not intermingle with the pre-industrial rural environment of the 18th and 19th centuries already re-created at the museum, their position close to the old homesteads will provide a valuable illustration of the historical links between the past and the present.

Chronological Table of Accessions

Name of Building	Place of Origin (p. = parish)	Acquired	Completed	Remarks	See page	Code on Map
Halland Farmstead Dwelling-house	Stämhult, Slätt-åkra p., Halland	1896	1897	Outbuildings, see below	72	A^a
east herberg of which	Ifås, Torup p., Halland	1896	1897			
Loft House	Kristvalla p., Småland	1896	1897		82	A^e
Näs Twin Farmstead	Norra Mellby p., Scania	1899	1901		86	A^f
Ostenfeld Farmstead	Ostenfeld, South Schleswig	1899	1901		164	F^e
Kiln or Bath-house	Gårdsby p., Småland	1907	1908		80	A^d
Fishermen's Hut	Nymindegab, Lønne p., West Jutland	1910	1910		199	G^c
Skipper's Cottage from Fanø	Sønderho, Fanø	1913	1915		190	G^a
Bole Barn from Grønninghoved	Grønninghoved, Vejstrup p., East Jutland (north Schleswig until 1864)	1918	1918		160	F^b
Splashmill	Mjölnetången, Gryteryd p., Småland	1920	1921		78	A^c
Post Mill	Karlstrup, Zealand	1921	1922		120	C^g
Fisherman's Cottage from Agger	Agger, West Jutland	1923	1925		208	G^e
Lundager Farmstead	Lundager, Gamtofte p., Funen	1924	1934	Two of the wings, though, were re-erected in 1926	130	E^a
Smallholder's Farmstead from Årup	Årup, Funen	1926	1935		139	E^c
Forge from Ørbæk	Ørbæk, Funen	1934	1936		136	E^b
Fuglevad Windmill	Fuglevad, Lyngby, Zealand	1937		In situ	96	C^a
Clogmaker's Cottage	Kirke-Søby, Funen	1936	1939		142	E^d
Skipper's Farmstead from Rømø	Toftum, Rømø	1935	1940		185	Fⁱ
Farmstead from True	True, Brabrand p., East Jutland	1930	1942		215	G^h
Farmstead from Karup Heath	Kølvrå, Grove p., Central Jutland	1932	1943		210	G^f
Pebringe Farmstead	Pebringe, Karise p., Zealand	1938-39	1945		96	C^b
Smallholder's Farmstead from Tågense	Tågense, Nysted landsogn (p.), Lolland	1928	1946		120	D^a
Halland Farmstead Outbuildings	Stråvalla p., Halland	1938-39	1949	Dwelling-house, see above	72	A^b
Farm Labourer's Cottage from Englerup	Englerup, Sonnerup p., Zealand	1946	1951		114	C^e

Name of Building	Place of Origin (p. = parish)	Acqui-red	Com-ple-ted	Remarks	See page	Code on Map
Fire Station	Kirke-Såby, Zealand	1936	1951		118	C^f
Potter's Workshop	Sorring, Dallerup p., East Jutland	1952	1954		212	G^g
Læsø Farmstead				Outbuildings, see below	222	G^j
Dwelling-house	Bangsbo, Hals p.,Læsø	1947	1955			
Post Mill	Byrum p., Læsø	1951	1955			
Dannemare Farmstead	Dannemare, Lolland	1950	1957		125	D^b
Weaver's Cottage	Tystrup, Zealand	1950	1958		109	C^d
Wheelwright's cottage	Kalvehave, Zealand	1944	1960		103	C^c
Eiderstedt Farmstead	Kating, Eiderstedt, South Schleswig	1956	1960		168	F^f
Watermill from Funen	Ellested p., Funen	1949	1964	Only dwelling-house and mill completed in 1964	148	E^e
Buildings from the Faroe Islands		1959 -61	1965	Replaced copy of Faroese house erected at museum in 1906	229	
Dwelling-house	Múla, Borðoy					H^a
Foodstore	Viðareiði, Viðoy					H^b
Kiln-house	Múla, Borðoy					H^c
Splashmill	Sandur, Sandoy					H^d
Manor-house Barn	Fjellerup, East Jutland	1952	1965		220	G^i
Farmstead from Vemb	Vemb, West Jutland	1961	1965	Regional museum farmstead taken over by the National Museum in 1930	202	G^d
Shoemaker's Cottage	Ødis Bramdrup, Ødis p., East Jutland (North Schleswig until 1864)	1962	1966		156	F^a
Lønnestak Farmstead	Lønnestak, Lønne p., West Jutland	1960	1967		193	G^b
Dörröd Cottage	Dörröd, Veberöd p., Scania	1965	1969		90	A^g
Watermill from Bornholm	Pedersker p., Bornholm	1952	1970		94	B^a
Læsø Farmstead				Dwelling-house, see above	222	G^j
Barn	Vesterø p., Læsø	1968	1971			
Byre	Bangsbo, Hals p.,Læsø	1968				
Farmstead from Sønder Sejerslev	Sønder Sejerslev, Emmerlev p., North Schleswig	1962	1971		174	F^g
Lace School	Nørre Sejerslev, Emmerlev p., North Schleswig	1965	1972		181	F^h
Bole Barn from Sparlund	Sparlund, Øsby p., North Schleswig	1930	1972		161	F^c
Dwelling-house from Barsø	Barsø, Løjt p., North Schleswig	1947		Re-erection begun in 1972	162	F^d

From House
to House

Village

It is virtually impossible to cover the entire museum during a single visit, and in order to decide which buildings to see, it is a good idea to find out where the cottages and farmsteads are situated in the museum park. And for this purpose there is a model of the museum in the entrance hall. Some, on the other hand, may simply prefer to walk through the park as the mood takes them.

Either way, however, the clear difference in the character of the settings will soon be noticed. Farmsteads are sometimes a distance away from each other scattered in open countryside. Elsewhere they cluster together in villages corresponding to their native environment. Not as close together as in towns, but with gardens between, or with space for a midden or a corn rick etc. In the past, though, farmsteads and cottages were often grouped so closely about the common land of the village that sometimes there were only narrow passages between the thatched buildings, and fire was an ever-present danger.

Bonds between neighbours were close in the peasant community of the past. Not only in cases of emergency, such as fire, was help forthcoming but also in everyday life. People helped each other with small jobs and worked jointly on the large ones. For example, the task of driving timber for a new building from the wood to the site was done by all, and likewise the roof construction and the wattle and daub walling. The completion of these jobs was celebrated by those who took part in the work. The cultivation of the fields at the time of the open-field system was also a common undertaking. Decisions on such collective matters were taken at the village meeting place – a circle of stones round a tree, each farmer sat on his own stone. Here, the affairs of the village were run; partly according to custom, partly according to stipulations or recommendations laid down by the authorities.

Left: This big lime tree with autumn tints is encircled by the stones of a village meeting place. It was usual for farmers in the era of the open field system to meet beneath a large tree in the middle of the village. The building in the foreground with open doors is the fire station. Fire fighting was one of the mutual matters which came up for discussion at a village meeting place.

Opposite page: The stones of the village meeting place from Funen are in a ring round a lime tree. Each farmer had his own stone to sit on when meetings were held to discuss village matters, for example when communal tasks should begin such as harvesting etc. The houses in the background are some of the museum's Funen buildings: the smallholder's cottage from Årup in front, and a corner of the clogmaker's cottage from Kirke-Søby behind.

Landscape with buildings from Lolland and Funen. The nearest is the farmstead from Tågense. At the centre is a village meeting place from Lolland: a circular platform of earth with a tree in the middle.

Countryside

Open countryside stretched before one's gaze in the old days once the cluster of farmsteads and cottages of a village was left behind. Close by was the patchwork of fields, and further away the uncultivated land or commons used for grazing. Nobody lived away from the villages in the times before the land reforms in the 1700's, and not a house would be seen between one village and the next. But after these reforms the land of each farm was gathered in compact holdings, and gradually more and more farmsteads were moved away from the villages to their fields. Little by little the landscape changed, villages were no longer as narrowly encompassed and sharply defined, and the

countryside between had a scattering of farmsteads.

However, there is also another type of open country in Denmark: the large tracts of infertile, thinly populated countryside in West and Central Jutland. Here there was not sufficient arable land to support large villages like those in the easterly regions, therefore farmsteads were usually dotted about the landscape or gathered in small groups with each farmstead at some distance from the next. A number of the buildings from Jutland at Frilandsmuseet comes from areas like these, and obviously must not be situated too close together. Their cultivated land was close to the farmstead, and usually they had one

Countryside created at Frilandsmuseet. A little stream winds from the pond towards the farmstead from Vemb. In the distance to the right can be seen the marshland farmstead.

or two meadows as well. They were otherwise surrounded by vast expanses of heath used for grazing, and where berries were picked. This landscape underwent a change in the 1800's when increasing areas of heath were reclaimed and more farmsteads sprang up. But it was still thinly populated.

At Frilandsmuseet the landscape in the northerly part of the park is intended to convey the open country in these parts of Jutland, but of course on a much smaller scale. Indeed, an illusion has to be conjured up at the museum. For example, a field seen from one angle is the setting for a manor house barn – the sweeping field characteristic of an estate – while from the opposite angle it is transformed into marshland tracts surrounding the Eiderstedt farmstead. Obviously only a hint of these landscapes is conveyed, and our difficulties in no way diminish when re-creating the landscape of East Denmark. There is not enough room to set the clusters of buildings in a setting of fields fringed in the distance by commons; this type of countryside cannot be experienced at the museum. But here and there throughout the terrain is a scattering of fields where crops are low and sparse, and where vetch and other almost forgotten weeds of the field intermingle among them.

Forest

Danish forests were so thoroughly exploited during the centuries immediately preceding the great land reforms that good forestland became a rarity, and the area of forested country gradually decreased. The era of land reforms in the 18th century, however, also brought about the beginning of organised forestry, and this combined with legislation on the protection of forests in 1805 resulted in the systematisation of foresty which saved the forests of Denmark.

In Frilandsmuseet are the remains of a forest which is extremely old. It is the stand of oak on the slope leading down to the river Mølleåen. It was described in 1660 as felled and desolate – an aftermath of the Swedish War when its trees had been cut down for timber. A new stand of oak grew up afterwards, some of the trees had even grown from the roots of the old oaks. These at any rate had roots which dated back to the Middle Ages. However, the oaks in the wood today are also worth tending with care: over 300 years old, they are contemporary with the oldest buildings in the museum, and give a tremendous perspective back in time. The position of the stand is also interesting, for it is preserved on the steep slope of the valley side which could not be ploughed, and ceases abruptly at the upper edge of the slope – a clearly defined limit when observed from the top.

The wood provides an interlude for those visiting the museum who, while strolling along the woodland path on

Boundary stone marking a royal hunting ground from Løvet in Central Jutland. On it is carved Christian VI's monogram with crown above, and the date 1743. S D stands for Skanderborg District, beneath is No. 10.

The chance of combining a museum visit with a country outing makes Frilandsmuseet what it is. This peaceful woodland path, for example, where nature must be enjoyed. But a little forest history can also be directly experienced.

their way to look at more old buildings, undoubtedly experience spontaneous pleasure from it, causing them to reflect perhaps on what forests have meant to the population in bygone days. The game preserve boundary stone tells us that this was the hunting ground of the king and noblemen. The wooden buildings at the museum reveal its other uses, although these were not restricted to building timber for enormous quantities of underwood and branches were needed for fencing and firewood. In most districts forests have also served primarily as a feeding ground for livestock. This unavoidably damaged the growth of new trees and underwood. The worst culprits were goats. The rootling of pigs among the trees, on the other hand, was often beneficial especially in beech forests.

At the middle of the 19th century onwards the area of forestland in Denmark increased enormously when extensive coniferous forests were planted, particularly in the heath districts. Stands of fir at Frilandsmuseet are to be found near the farmsteads which come from heathland districts.

The forest at Frilandsmuseet supplies timber which is dressed with a broad-axe in the old-fashioned way. It is then used when the old houses are re-erected and timbers sometimes have to be renewed.

Roads and Bridges

Frilandsmuseet is for pedestrians only. Now and again the question of building a road for cars is raised, but this would in many ways be an unfortunate innovation. For those who are not able to walk very far a horse drawn wagon is available. Horses' hooves and the crunch of wheels on gravel has an old-fashioned sound, but all other heavy traffic would be disturbing. Besides, a quiet walk along the roads in the museum gives visitors time to enjoy details in the landscape and the changing impressions of the buildings. Sometimes, though, even a road has a story to tell.

Horse-drawn cart with museum visitors on their way through the East Jutland village.

Admittedly, there are no examples at
the museum of the most primitive road –
wheel tracks threading their way through
the countryside. Roads at the museum
have a firm gravel surface, and they are the
type which became usual during the latter
half of the 18th century along important
routes. The upkeep of these roads was
often shared by the people living beside
them, and the divisions were sometimes
marked by special boundary stones,
examples of which can be seen in a couple
of places by the roadside at Frilandsmuseet. The sunken road leading down to the
watermill from Funen is an excellent illustration of an ancient road. It is of course
far older than the museum itself, and originally led down to a ford which has long
since disappeared. A crossing of this kind
over a watercourse has not been made at
the museum. On the other hand, a bridge
of heavy, hewn pieces of granite has been
re-erected.

Not far from this bridge, where a road
passes through some heath, is a stone on
a little mound. The three holes in it denote
a measure of distance, each hole representing a *fjerding* – an old measure, approximately a mile. Milestones of this type
date back to the first large-scale mapping
of highways in Denmark undertaken
during the last half of the 17th century.
There are other types of milestone along
the roads in the museum.

*Left: The three small holes in this milestone denote a mea-
sure of distance, each hole representing a fjerdingvej (¼
Danish mile or 1 English mile). It stands on a small
mound, the usual position for old milestones dating back
to the close of the 1600's.*

*Opposite: Granite bridge from the Holstebro district in
northerly West Jutland. It now spans a stream running
past a farmstead from the same region.*

This corner of garden belonging to the Årup farmstead gives an impression of the profusion of Funen gardens. Decorative hollyhocks by the walls of the cottage, and to the right a green tangle of hop vines.

Gardens

Not all countryfolk had gardens in the old days. Some districts were so windswept and infertile that only the most hardy plants could survive. And not all of those of humble means had enough land to spare for a garden. However, even in the most barren districts a few vegetables were grown. This was in every sense of the word a cabbage patch, for in many places cabbages were the only vegetable, although several varieties were often cultivated together.

It is indeed a far cry from the simplest cabbage patch to the luxuriant flower gardens of some of the farmsteads at the museum which come from areas with altogether better conditions for gardening.

The gardens from Funen are among the most highly developed with an abundance of different species in both the vegetable and flower gardens. The strict geometrical divisions of the flower beds are an old custom, but they also illustrate how the fashions of the upper classes spread to simpler homes. For example, the garden landscaping found in bygone days in monasteries and manor houses survives in cottage gardens. It is a combination of imitation and a direct influence, in that people in authority – particularly during the period of land reforms – made efforts to encourage the peasantry to have gardens. Thus, already by the middle of the 15th century, the peasants of the island

70

of Lolland were commanded to grow apple and pear trees by their homesteads.

Many of the gardens at Frilandsmuseet are laid out according to what is generally known about the development of gardens, but quite a number corresponds closely to the original garden. In the latter case the old garden has been measured, and its species of plants recorded, and seeds and cuttings taken back to the museum to enable the setting to be reproduced as faithfully as possible.

Livestock

In the chapters on the history of Frilandsmuseet various plants have been mentioned, particularly in connection with the recent extensions to the museum park which enabled greater attention to be paid to details of the landscape, for example the planting of native species to correspond to the locality of the farmstead. And in the following, too, remarks will fall here and there to explain why lyme-grass is to be found in some parts of the museum and, for example, why ash thickets preponderate elsewhere. But why should the museum keep horses, bullocks, heifers, sheep, goats, geese, chickens and pigeons?

As we have mentioned before, animals simply add an extra touch of the countryside to the settings – bringing them to life. This should not be interpreted to mean that the museum aims to conceal the fact that the old buildings are museum exhibits, and as such lifeless relics of past milieux. To the contrary, they are interesting because of it for we cannot find homes like them elsewhere now. Animals are very much part of the qualities which combine to make an open-air museum both recreative and educational with a charm of its own. And there is no doubt that farm animals help to pacify small children, and give young parents an opportunity to study the old buildings more closely.

Apart from keeping the museum's young visitors amused, the animals give town children a closer glimpse of the most important livestock of a farm, and at a higher level illustrate what an enormous role they played in the rural economy of the past. This can be seen in all the farmsteads and cottages at the museum, not only in the cowsheds, stables and coach-houses, but also in the sculleries where dairying and slaughtering were done, and in the dwelling-rooms where sheep's wool was spun, and where the family slept under quilts stuffed with goose feathers.

A flock of geese at the edge of the village pond. Behind is the red-washed forge from Funen. The cackle of geese has a countrified sound in the ears of visitors to the museum. When the geese grow so large that small children become afraid of them, they are moved to a fenced paddock nearby where they can be watched from a safe distance.

The Halland Farmstead

As the Halland farmstead stands today on its hill-side in the middle of Frilandsmuseet, it is one of the buildings in the museum which conveys the strongest sense of atmosphere to visitors. The dark timber walls impart a feeling of age and strangeness. One walks through the covered gateway into a flag-paved courtyard and up the stone steps to the terrace on which the dwelling-house is situated. It is almost with awe that one passes through the low entrance into the gloom beyond. Indeed, in sunny weather it takes a little time before the eyes grow accustomed to the shadow within.

The unfailing enchantment of the Halland farmstead was also presumably experienced by Bernhard Olsen, the founder of the museum, when he decided to acquire the dwelling-house. But it is unlikely that he ever imagined that one day the farmstead would be assembled as it is today in its magnificent entirety.

Both in Kongens Have and later, for many years, in Sorgenfri, the wings containing farm buildings were absent. However, the dwelling-house alone – the Halland dwelling as it was called – was in itself an exciting building. It fully satisfied Bernhard Olsen's requirements for a very old house, which could clearly reveal something about earlier phases in the evolution of the dwelling.

Perhaps the best known feature is the open fireplace with a fine coved mantle over the hearth. It was taken as the motif for a poster by the artist Sikker Hansen in 1951, and the poster became the most sought after one in the range of posters commissioned by the museum. It helped to make the open fireplace popular as well. Indeed, among the visitors to the museum there were some who did not only hang up the poster in their homes, but who also built a similar fireplace with considerable difficulty in their week-end cottages.

The fireplace, however, is not as old as the building itself. It was probably built during the course of the 18th century. This part of the dwelling-house, though, dates from the 17th century and was originally heated by an open hearth at floor level. This is before chimneys became usual, and smoke from the hearth simply passed through a hole in the roof – a louver. Therefore, the only window in this room is in the roof, a relic of early times when the only light to seep into the interior came from the louver.

The Halland dwelling was not selected solely because of its hearth detail. The construction of the building as a whole argued in favour of its selection, for it is divided into three parts. The middle part is the lowest building, but the room inside fills the whole interior from floor to ridge. This is the part comprising the living room, and the only room which could be heated. It is clearly here the more peaceful indoor pursuits took place. All the other rooms must have been bitterly cold in the winter. Meals were eaten here, either close to the fireplace where the food was cooked, or at a table by the gable wall; the occupants of the house slept here, some in alcove beds and others on the benches along the wall.

A little single room dwelling of this kind was most likely the living quarters in a number of Halland farmsteads a few centuries ago. However, other buildings were added at an early date to the original

Previous page: The Halland farmstead is high-lying compared to the road. Only the outbuildings can be seen from this angle. All their walls are of wood, either horizontal bole planks or upright boards. The thatched roof is very familiar, only the stone sill and stone walling give a feeling of a slightly strange milieu – a region with an abundance of stones.

The Halland dwelling-house is in three parts. In the middle is a low room with a chimney, it is flanked by a taller unit on each side: so-called herbergs. The roof is turf covered in contrast to the thatched outbuildings, and the courtyard is paved with flagstones. In front of the dwelling-house is a strip of garden supported by a dry stone wall with room for a couple of beehives, some herbs and flowers.

house in most places, thereby enlarging the dwelling as demonstrated by the museum's exhibit.

The three-part dwelling-house has a so-called *herberg* on either side of the lower house. The herbergs are unheated, they have ceilings and lofts for storage. Their storage capacity is a primary function, but they were also working rooms. For example, rough domestic work was carried out there, and in one of the museum's herbergs can be seen items normally found in a scullery – large vessels and utensils used when food has to be preserved for a long period.

In the other herberg are the tools used for making textiles. Spinning was probab-

ly done near the warmth of the hearth in the low house, but it was not easy to move round with the loom, and the women undoubtedly sat out in the herberg when weaving. A certain amount of completed fabric and clothing was kept in the chests here. The alcove beds in this herberg show that not everyone slept in the middle room, and additional sleeping accommodation was provided – primarily for servants or large offspring.

The three-part dwelling-house was a type which interested Bernhard Olsen, and the Halland dwelling had to be of this type at all costs. For contemporary research into rural building traditions had already drawn attention to this curious form of building widespread in South Sweden. Later scholars have also found that this composite building form clearly confirms a theory of the development of long-houses. The wings of Danish and Scanian farmsteads, according to this theory, were in fact originally small houses built in continuation of each other. Further south these small houses fused together better due to the half-timbering technique which used short timbers. The Halland dwelling, however, was built of fir logs laid horizontally and depended in consequence on the length of the fir trunks, and this explains why each phase of the building maintained its character as an independent unit.

Seen in this light, it must have vexed Bernhard Olsen somewhat that one of the herbergs of the dwelling-house he had chosen for removal had been renewed. The Halland dwelling comes from Stämhult, Slättåkra parish north of Halmstad, and the renewed east herberg was replaced by one from a neighbouring locality – Ifås in Torup parish.

For many years visitors to the museum received but a faint impression of the occupational background of the curious Halland dwelling. As time passed the incomplete farmstead was felt to be more and more unsatisfactory, and towards the close of the Thirties steps were taken to complete it. A provisional agreement to take over three wings of farm buildings was arranged, but the war intervened and the plans had to be suspended. Not until 1949 could the complete Halland farmstead be opened to the public with its

wings from a farm in Stråvalla parish midway between Varberg and Kungsbacka. These farm buildings enclose three sides of the courtyard; they contain a series of rooms which gives an excellent impression of how the Halland peasants subsisted. Barn, cowshed, stable and pigsty alternate so that fodder did not have to be transported far, and necessary small repairs were carried out in the workshop. Some of the farming implements were simple and home-made, for example the so-called *fällekratta* or hand harrow was barely fashioned at all, simply a root end with some small lateral branches at one end. It was used to break up and level lumpy soil after burning, as well as to cover the seed after sowing. It tells a tale of centuries of toil better than much else.

The addition of farm buildings to the old Halland dwelling-house not only sheds better light on the existence of peasants in that area in former times, but also on its building traditions. While the dwelling-house is constructed in the horizontal log technique with corner joints, the outbuildings have walls timbered with heavy horizontal boards laid in grooves in the upright posts – the timber is either oak or pine – in the bole-house technique. In contrast to the turf covered roof of the dwelling-house, the three wings are thatched in the usual manner, and the roofs partly supported by some tall posts beneath the ridge. This kind of post is called a ridge post from which the term "ridge post construction" is derived.

The fact that the Halland farmstead has been pieced together from buildings in different localities does not necessarily mean it is in anyway impaired. In this particular case it is because when the buildings were acquired by the museum no complete farmstead of this type could be found in a good state of preservation in Halland.

75

It is sometimes an advantage for the museum not to be bound by the fortuitous structural features of a single farmstead. A composite farmstead, like this example from Halland, on the other hand, can result in a complex of buildings which corresponds to what was once representative of an area. A prerequisite for this being that local building traditions and interior arrangements are thoroughly investigated.

Opposite page: The fireplace is the focal point of the dwelling. Food was cooked here and it provided warmth. A good place to sit was close to the fire, and in the Halland room it was also the lightest spot being just beneath the skylight. In the evenings light came from a burning splint of resinous pine in a pine light holder standing beside the little table. In the background between the chimney and dresser can be glimpsed one of the herbergs containing large household vessels.

Below: The herberg has a ceiling. Unlike the low dwelling-room, light comes in through a window in the wall. Weaving was done in the herberg by the women, their other handicrafts can also be seen. Fabric and clothing of various kinds were stored in chests. The one in the middle has a painted decoration and the date 1787. The room is also decorated with a long valance of patterned fabric along the top of the walls.

Splashmill from Småland

Small watermills of this type were used either by one farm or a limited number of farms. In any event, the amount of corn that could be ground was relatively restricted by their size, which made them unsuitable for districts with a heavy grain production.

Indeed, the watermill could well have belonged to the Halland farmstead although it is from Småland, however its native locality was a mere kilometre or two from the boundary to Halland, directly east of Varberg, in Mjölnetången in the parish of Gryteryd.

It is one of the smallest buildings in the museum – only a few metres in each direction – built of horizontal fir logs interlocking at the corners in the alternating groove technique. The roof is of shingles.

The term "splashmill" is often used to describe a little mill of this type. This is possibly because only a splash of water is necessary to turn its wheels, or perhaps because the word describes the gentle splashing sound it gives. Yet the term is also used for certain windmills. It gives no hint of how mills bearing the name are constructed, nor what kind of milling they were used for.

The Småland splashmill is a watermill with a horizontal wheel, i.e. the water wheel rotates horizontally, and water runs down the sloping sluice hitting one side of the water wheel, thus driving the mill. The upper millstone is attached to the top end of the shaft driven by the water wheel. It is a very simple mechanical device: the water wheel and millstone always turn at the same speed because they are attached to the same shaft.

For many years after the erection of the watermill at the museum in 1921 a fair measure of imagination was necessary in order to understand how it worked, for it was situated on dry land and the sluice was so broad that running water would have hit both sides of the wheel. The more reflective members of the public must have pondered over this, although not all of them wrote to the museum like the Nobel prizewinner August Krogh. In 1969 the watermill was turned slightly and a stream led to it so it could once again spin round.

Opposite page: The splashmill from Småland straddles a stream. The lower works of the mill merge into the gloom beneath the building. Water runs down to the mill through a sloping wooden trough on the other side of the building. Behind this, up the hill, the little stream is stemmed by a sluice-gate. This is opened when water is to be diverted to the mill. The watermill turns almost constantly when the museum is open.

Left: Since the enlargement the central clearing is no longer at the centre of the museum, it is situated close to the splashmill. There is a kiosk and a picnic place with tables and benches in the sun or in the shade. An oasis where refreshments can be had, and one of the few places in the museum park where smoking is permitted. Smoking is otherwise obviously strictly prohibited.

Kiln or Bath-House

This small building is one of the three buildings in the museum from Småland which have rather a special function. It can be said of them all that at the time they were acquired by the museum, the preference would have been to collect them from one of the old Danish provinces: Scania, Halland – perhaps most of all from Blekinge, which was not represented. This viewpoint was not influenced by a preoccupation with national history but rather with cultural history, and satisfaction was felt over the fact that buildings could be acquired in Småland which were not to be found nearer at hand.

In this case the "bath-house" was collected from Kråkenäs in Gårdsby parish just north of Växjö, well into Småland, consequently it is not surprising that the charac-teristic construction of the great coniferous regions of Scandinavia is demonstrated in this building, like all the others from Småland.

The walls are built of horizontal fir logs with corner joints lightly mortised; this forms a kind of knot and it may be the reason why the technique is called *knuttimring* in Swedish. In Danish it is called *knudetømring,* but the term is rarely used. On the other hand, the word *blokhus* has been used by military builders for the same construction, and more recently the term has spread to describe holiday chalets built like log cabins. The Norwegian term *laftebygge* is also sometimes used. The general uncertainty about the name of this construction in Denmark is because the technique is not indigenous, but, on the other hand, the natural method of construction in the coniferous regions of the rest of Scandinavia. The technique was used in parts of the former Danish landscapes of Halland, in northern Scania, and in Blekinge.

When calling this small log built house with roof of turf a bath-house, it really ought to be qualified by the word "so-called". Most buildings of this kind in South Sweden were primarily used for drying purposes. Steam baths, though, have a longer tradition in Sweden than for example in Denmark. A number of bath-houses in Sweden were used for various forms of bathing and washing until fairly recently.

It had a variety of uses in its chief capacity as a drying kiln, for example the drying of flax, malt and grain, although the most common was presumably flax drying, which in turn meant that other

Frilandsmuseet is a peaceful spot for wild animals. Visitors enjoy this. It is not unusual to see a red squirrel in one of the trees, and there is a rich birdlife. But only the fortunate will see a fox when the museum is open.

The bath-house is a good example of the building traditions in the coniferous regions of Scandinavia. The walls are of fir logs with corner joints. The roof is covered with turf except for the porch roof which is of boards. The murky interior has a stove on one wall, and broad shelves along the other walls. The shelter in front of the door was used for storing fuel and other items.

tasks connected with the preparation of flax was carried out either in or near the kiln. Those working with it often sat beneath the planking roof of the porchlike shelter at the gable.

When the bath-house was acquired by the museum in 1908 there were probably three reasons which particularly influenced the choice: it was associated with the supposedly ancient tradition of steam bathing in Scandinavia, it represented a simple, old-fashioned type of building consisting of a single room, with a shelter beneath the overhanging roof, and lastly,

it had a primitive stove common to this type of kiln which was of interest. It warmed the interior so that the flax etc. could be dried on the broad shelves along the walls. It was a kind of coved smoke stove with no chimney, the smoke found its way out through the opening in the front through which it was fuelled.

In other words, the oven was stoked in the same way as many of the bread ovens in the old buildings at the museum. But little is known of the other uses of ovens of this kind. To date in Denmark, our knowledge is theoretical and based on archaeological material. Comparisons have been drawn between it and the smoke oven for heating, encountered until fairly recently in certain parts of Norway.

The Loft House

The last of the three buildings from Småland is the loft house, it was the first of them to be acquired by the museum in 1896 and re-erected on the first site in Kongens Have, and opened to the public the following year. It was among the buildings that could be seen when the museum re-opened in 1901 after moving to Lyngby.

The loft house comes from a farmstead called Åbro in the parish of Kristvalla, situated north-west of Kalmar not far from the town of Nybro. Bernhard Olsen never concealed where the building came from in his reports. It is very possible that he would have liked the building to represent the Blekinge region. In any event, the museum maintained somewhat over-strenuously for many years after his time the myth that it came from the border between Blekinge and Småland. This was a trifle disingenuous considering that its native locality was between 25 and 30 miles from the border as the crow

flies. In this light, then, the designation given the Småland watermill on signs and in guidebooks was better justified, i.e. that it came from the Halland border.

The loft house at the museum looks very Swedish indeed, especially since receiving a red colour-wash a few years ago after traces had been found showing that it had earlier been this colour. The colour pigment used was first introduced in Småland in the 17th century, it became usual during the course of the following century, and all-dominating in the 19th century.

Although it is evident that the loft house was not painted red as soon as it was built, it could well have been, because it is unlikely to be older than c.1700. An idea of the age of a construction of this kind can be gained from the manner in which the fir baulks have been fashioned. Norwegian and Swedish scholars of building traditions have studied the methods in detail, for the way in which timbers were dressed was very much subject to fashion and useful for dating purposes in consequence.

Other features of loft houses, moreover, have undergone slight variations in the course of time. For example, the enclosed balcony of the loft house at the museum is an early feature which tells us a little about the age of the building, likewise the finely-shaped wooden balusters across the balcony aperture, and the triangular

Opposite page: The loft house has two storerooms below, each with its own door. The outside stairway leads to a closed balcony. Behind are two empty rooms with no door between. Threshed corn was probably stored here. With its red colour-wash the loft house looks very Swedish. The fence is intended to convey its native origin.

Left: There are many kinds of enclosures at Frilandsmuseet. The stone wall enclosing a paddock by the farmstead from Scania is characteristic of its native region. At the museum the paddock is also used by cattle.

82

One of the storerooms in the loft house is used for storing flour, butter and cheese. The large bins are for flour. Utensils for baking and cheese making etc. are kept here.

border along the lower timbers of the balcony projection.

Bernhard Olsen's determination to have a loft house like this in the museum is curious – there is an alien air about it. But the fact that it was torn from its native setting caused little concern, as in those days it was not so much the function of buildings but rather whether they represented a certain type in the evolutionary sequence that mattered. Nevertheless, Bernhard Olsen did not fit the loft house directly into the simple sequence he was otherwise concerned with, although it was the significance of the loft house in the general context of the development of rural building traditions, which provided him with the reason for acquiring this strange building.

The first guidebook to the museum expresses the reason clearly, for in it the loft house is compared with the "high loft" and bower of medieval folk songs. Hence the Småland loft house was intended to represent a type of building supposed to have been widespread throughout the North. It served as a storehouse and sometimes as a sleeping place – for women, servants or guests.

Recent research can in many ways substantiate this conception of former years; thus in the light of modern criteria, too, the presence of this exciting red, timber building at Frilandsmuseet is fully justified and not, as one could easily suspect, a romantic flight of fancy. For it is now considered that the loft house has some link with a form of two-storey building which has long been one of the elements

There is a special room on the ground floor of the loft house for storing meat. Implements for slaughtering are kept here. Cranberries are stored in the jar in the foreground.

in rural architecture including that in Denmark. Namely a building which could not be heated, primarily used for stores but sometimes as sleeping quarters.

There is now nothing in the museum's loft house from Småland to indicate whether it was used for sleeping in, but this may well have been the case, because a number of similar Småland buildings contain sleeping accommodation in their upper storey. Although it is most likely that the loft was used for storing grain as in many other farmsteads in that part of Småland.

As mentioned earlier, the rooms in the loft house were not furnished and arranged in keeping with the museum's interior

principles when it was re-erected, but some years ago the two rooms on the ground floor were equipped with the belongings and tools usually found in rooms of this kind. Some of the items even came from the farmstead to which the loft house had belonged, and also from other farmsteads in the neighbourhood.

The two rooms demonstrate how the storehouse of a Småland farmstead was equipped in bygone days when these farmsteads were virtually self-supporting. In one room are bins for flour, butter, cheese etc., as well as utensils for baking and cheese-making. In the other room are barrels and hooks for storing preserved meat, as well as slaughtering implements. Here, too, are jars of cranberries and juniper-berries which were an important constituent of the daily diet.

The Näs Twin Farmstead

The son of the house related many years afterwards how, one Sunday in 1899, a Dane drove up to the double farmstead. The visitor was a big, sturdy man with a grey beard and he wanted to buy the farm. This Dane happened to be Bernhard Olsen, who, with the acquisition of this large twin farmstead, secured one of the most important buildings for the coming museum of buildings in Lyngby. When the museum was inaugurated two years later on Midsummer Day 1901, one of Bernhard Olsen's achievements was the fact that the farmstead had been re-erected and already stood at the northernmost end of the original museum park.

The place-name Näs designates both farmstead and locality. It is situated in Norra Mellby parish in V. Göinge *herred*

The dwelling-houses of the Näs twin farmstead are built in extension of each other. They look like a row of small terrace houses, but only the lower whitewashed buildings can be heated.

(approx. county) in the middle of northerly Scania. It is still a well-wooded region, in contrast to the plains of south-west Scania, the predominant species being deciduous. This is the geographical factor which explains the construction of the farmstead: the so-called bole technique that is characteristic of the region, and which necessitated an ample supply of oak.

The special feature of bole-houses is that their walls are built of heavy horizontal oak boards with the ends mortised into the dividing uprights. This type of house has presumably once been found throughout virtually the whole of Denmark. However, in more recent times, it has survived in only certain areas, i.e. South-East Jutland, North Scania as well as Halland and Blekinge.

A large building complex like the twin farmstead from Näs, built entirely of timber, conveys an immediate impression of solidity and protection. In order to correct this notion, it should perhaps be added that a farm labourer who had been employed by both farmers, later recalled above all else how cold it had been indoors. The reason he never truly froze was because he slept with horse blankets over him. His quarters were in the little outhouse in the corner of the courtyard abutting the south wing. Here, it was not only cold but the roof leaked, and it rained in on him. This description can be believed but with a modicum of reservation as it dates from the time the two steadings were falling into disrepair,

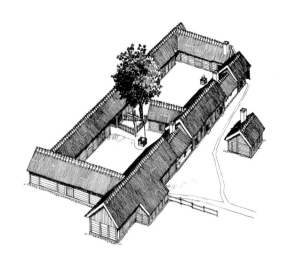

A drawing of the two complex adjoining Näs steadings gives a clear idea of their lay-out. A corner of the courtyard of the western steading can be seen in the photograph below. The whitewashed building is the oldest and dates from 1688. On each side of the low white building with a chimney is a taller unheated herberg used for storage purposes and rough indoor work.

shortly before it became possible for the museum to buy them. But it was not unusual for the rooms of farm labourers to be somewhat unpleasant to live in.

The temperature of the room on the other side in the south wing was not particularly clement either. It was a herberg, an unheated room used as a storeroom, but also sometimes for sleeping in. In the Näs farmstead the herberg is situated in the middle of a row of rooms because the dwelling-houses here are in continuation of each other.

Each of the two families had a kitchen-living room but the rest of the rooms were unheated. These low living rooms are easily recognisable from the outside because they are whitewashed and have chimneys, while the timber of the other buildings is untreated. However, the kitchen–living rooms have not always had chimneys for

they date back to the time when one managed without.

The age of these two oldest parts of the twin farmstead is very tangible, for the oak planks of the walls are unusually thick and extend from corner-post to corner-post. There is, moreover, a piece of evidence which bears this out. On the north-east corner-post of the western steading is carved the date 1688. Over the door of the eastern steading is likewise a date: 1737.

Apart from the considerable age of the steadings, the other buildings are also generally old, and although the wings are not all equally old they undoubtedly date well back into the 18th century. Moreover, the arrangement of the rooms within the buildings is not any later. It is easy to understand why every effort was made in the early years of the museum's existence to acquire this farmstead in order to re-create an early phase in the history of dwellings.

The old farmstead was unusually well preserved, although of course a certain amount of modernisation had been under-

taken. For example, extra space had been gained by building a bread oven so that it protruded from the outside wall. When the re-erection took place at the museum an earlier custom, known in other farmsteads, was followed, whereby the bread oven is kept entirely within the walls of the building. The walls of the dwelling-houses had been concealed inside by a later covering of boards and wallpaper. Bernhard Olsen has described a solemn moment during the dismantling process: "When we pulled these decorations down, the roof of the old room re-appeared – sooty and black from centuries of hearth smoke."

Bernhard Olsen succeeded in acquiring

The cowshed in the west Näs steading is very simple. Partitions between the stalls are low and there is no drain. This was not very necessary in the times before beets were introduced as fodder.

a collection of furniture from the neighbourhood of the farmstead which was not only old, but in many cases echoed still earlier traditions. Here were sleeping benches with cushions, and a bed of the same type as that known from the Viking period. If one were distinguished enough to merit a place at the "high" table, one could partake of a festive meal which even a former stage decorator like Bernhard Olsen would have experienced difficulty in arranging.

Left: The long north side of the Näs twin farmstead could first be seen by visitors to the museum in the 1960's. Before this the museum boundary was only a few metres from the wall which was hidden by a hedge. In front of the gateway which once led out into the fields from the east steading now stands a hay cart from Scania.

The Dörröd Cottage

Of the buildings in the museum whose origins are east of the Sound, this smallholder's cottage is the last to be acquired. It was purchased in 1965, dismantled the following year, and opened to the public at the museum in 1969. Like most of the other buildings acquired by the museum, the staff of the museum had in fact known about the cottage for a number of years prior to its purchase. But the decision had been taken not to move it, one of the reasons being that some experts felt it resembled buildings from Zealand too closely. Curiously enough, it was this very resemblance which was one of the later arguments in favour of its acquisition. For the close cultural links between the regions on each side of the Sound could be illustrated at the museum with the help of this cottage: fortunate indeed that it still existed by the time this fact was acknowledged.

The Dörröd from which the cottage comes is in South-West Scania, about 10 miles south-east of Lund, on the easterly escarpment of the Romele esker. This area is the transitional zone between the building traditions of the plain to the south-west and those of the forestland to the north-east. The building traditions of the transitional zone, however, more closely resemble those of the plain where half-timbering with an in-filling of wattle and daub has for centuries been the usual rural building method. Therefore, buildings in this region often vary considerably in appearance from those of the forested areas where plentiful timber left its mark on building traditions.

Yet Frilandsmuseet solely possessed buildings from the richly wooded areas of Scania until the acquisition of the Dörröd cottage. Even though the bole construction has also been widespread in Denmark, the amount of timber used, say, in

Opposite page: Seen from this angle the Dörröd cottage could well be a Zealand homestead, but in South-West Scania farmsteads closely resemble those in Zealand. A stream flows past close to the gables of the cottage as on its native site.

The dwelling-room of the Dörröd cottage has many local details, for example the black stone slab as a table top, and on the folding bed is a counterpane woven in a Scanian pattern.

Previous page: Above the stove in the dwelling-room of the Dörröd cottage is a drying rack for clothes. On the wall above the armchair is a framed paper memorial.

the twin farmstead from Göinge *herred*, may seem a little overwhelming to the modern Dane. It could also mislead visitors to the museum into thinking that the folk culture of Scania has been somewhat alien. In addition, the twin farmstead was furnished and equipped in a very old-fashioned way, and a very natural desire to represent a slightly later phase in the cultural development of Scania began to take shape. Also from the point of view of social divisions it was called for, because the twin farmstead indisputably represented the environment of the farmer

while the Dörröd cottage tells us a little about the rather more humble existence of the smallholder.

It is difficult to say anything definite about the age of this cottage as its construction is one which has been customary for many generations. But we do know quite a lot about who lived in it. On the other hand, it cannot be seen from old records when in the course of the 18th century the former cottage on the site disappeared, and the later cottage (the one now at the museum) was built. But it is clear that originally the building was not as large as it is now. About 1800 it comprised only two wings at right-angles, but during the middle of the 19th century the third wing was added, giving the cottage the same appearance as it has now.

The reason for enlarging the cottage was presumably because its occupiers received more land to work and needed more outbuilding space. The farming carried out by this family was by no means extensive, either during the time it was a copyholding or later, as an independent smallholding, for a family could scarcely live off the 1½-2½ acres belonging to it. The father of the family had to go out to work for others. At the middle of the 19th century, however, the addition of a little more land brought better times to the smallholding which then amounted to 8-9 acres. It was still not much, and the owner at that period was also a tailor as well as smallholder. Later, conditions worsened again when some of the land was sold, and the last occupant, a widow, lived in extremely humble circumstances. When re-creating the interior of the cottage, the museum has sought the period prior to this last era of decline. On the basis of inventories for probate, which list in detail everything in the cottage, it is now furnished and equipped as it had been about the year 1880. At that time it was still a normal household with enough land to farm to enable the outbuildings to be used for their proper purpose.

Watermill from Bornholm

Right down in the south-easterly corner of Frilandsmuseet is one of the smallest buildings in the museum. It is a watermill which originally came from Pedersker parish in southern Bornholm. It was dismantled in 1952 and opened at the museum in 1970.

The mill belonged to a single farm and was situated by a stream just below it. Similarly at the museum there are plans one day to re-erect a farmstead from Bornholm on the slope above it. However, the watermill is so far the only building to represent the island of Bornholm at the museum. A heavy burden for such a modest building, for Bornholm is in

In the oldest of the wings is a threshing floor beside the barn at the end of the central wing. At the gable of the oldest wing is a little stable. We know exactly how much livestock the occupiers had in 1874: a horse, a cow, a heifer, a calf, two sheep with lambs and a sow with piglets.

The latter were not in the stable but in the wing which was added later. There was also room for chickens beside the pigsty, as well as storage space for a cart, and a hand grinding mill. This part of the wing also served as a woodshed. The wing did not adjoin the dwelling-house and a narrow passage separates them, probably because the well behind had to be reached from the kitchen.

The kitchen had an open chimney, like the Zealand type, which was so roomy that the person cooking actually stood inside the chimney. The bread oven protruding from the back of the house was stoked from here, as well as the iron stove in the dwelling room. This stove bearing the name of King Carl XIII of Sweden, the rag carpet in the loom and the boarded façade remind us, that in spite of its familiar appearance, the cottage comes from Sweden.

many ways an exciting and characteristic area with regard to its rural building traditions. Some of the Bornholm features are evident in the watermill, for example the in-filling of sandstone between the half-timbering.

In its capacity as a mill, too, this little building is of importance as it illustrates one of the main types of watermill used in Denmark in the past. The big wheel beneath the gable is a so-called undershot wheel. Mechanically speaking it is not a particularly complicated system. Power is transferred through simple gearing to the upper stone of the mill situated in the loft.

Opposite page: The gable of the watermill from Bornholm projects over the large mill wheel.

Fuglevad Windmill

This mill differs from all the other buildings in Frilandsmuseet by virtue of the fact that it has never been moved. It has stood in the same position since it was built in 1832. It functioned as a grain mill until the beginning of the present century.

At the same time as Frilandsmuseet was installed on the neighbouring plot of land, it was apparently about to become obsolete. Already in 1901 the windmill was offered for sale to the museum, but nothing came of the offer. A few years later the mill was abandoned and soon fell into serious disrepair. The unguarded mill was a source of considerable anxiety to the museum, because a fire in this large building would have put the neighbouring Ostenfeld farmstead in grave danger.

At one point the windmill was about to be pulled down. This move was for-

tunately prevented when a private citizen with an interest in mills bought it and had it restored, after which he donated it to the Agricultural Museum in 1918. It was not until 1937 that the windmill was taken over by Frilandsmuseet.

The history of Fuglevad windmill is fairly characteristic. It was built at a time when farming in Denmark concentrated primarily on cereals. Many windmills were erected during the first half of the 19th century, and these were all so-called Dutch mills. In this type of windmill only the cap carrying the sails turns to the wind, whereas in the post mill type the entire mill can be revolved according to the direction of the wind.

The Pebringe Farmstead

There are three factors which have particularly contributed towards making this farmstead known, even among people who have never seen it. Extensive excavations were carried out on the site after the buildings had been removed, moreover the distinguished Danish author Martin A. Hansen has written about the farm, and last but not least it was re-erected at the museum according to a special method whereby all its irregularities were faithfully reproduced.

We should perhaps turn first to the excavations. By the end of the Thirties it was generally acknowledged that a serious hiatus existed in the research on the history of habitation in Denmark. Iron Age dwellings had been excavated by archeologists in various heathland regions of Jutland, but no prehistoric habitations had been found in Zealand. What had hap-

pened to the Iron Age peasants whose dwellings were excavated centuries later beneath drift sand and heather? Were they perhaps the first peasants of the villages, the age of which place-name scholars were able to shed light on? In other words, the time was ripe to carry out an excavation beneath an existing farmstead, and the opportunity arose when Frilandsmuseet moved the Pebringe farmstead from South-East Zealand to the museum.

The intention was to take the existing buildings as the point of departure for the excavation in the hope of clarifying their immediate past, and perhaps to explain some of the features of their ground-plan. And indeed this was an important result of the excavation. In any event, the area near the hearth yielded some information about the predecessor to the present dwelling-house. Traces were also found of buildings dating back to the Middle Ages,

Previous page: *A cart stands in the gateway of the Pebringe farmstead ready to be used in the fields when crops were brought in to the barn on each side of the gateway. Four adjoining whitewashed wings enclose the courtyard; there are outshots here and there, shown in the drawing to the right. The dwelling-house is opposite the gateway. The slightly crooked row of windows illustrates the painstaking preservation of the building's irregularities which typifies this farmstead.*

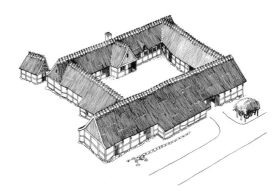

possibly to c. 1300, beneath the wings housing the stables and barn. This, then, gave reasonable grounds to support the theory of continuous habitation on the site back through the ages. On the other hand, no link could be proved between the traces found beneath the buildings of dwellings from the last centuries B.C. and the later ones.

Hearths from the different phases of habitation, however, were of great significance during the excavation, for they are among the features of a building which leave the clearest traces in the soil. In addition, the hearth is undeniably an important part of a building, particularly in northern climes because it makes a building habitable.

It is hardly surprising that the large open chimney attracted Martin A. Hansen so greatly. In his description of the Pebringe farmstead it played the dominant role. That he attached importance to these thoughts of bygone days, "old life" as he called it, is illustrated by the fact that his "thoughts in a chimney" provided the title for the entire book (1948). He describes the great size of the chimney, and mentions how the fireplace – the hearth – was always at the centre of the dwelling: the heart of this old Zealand farmstead. The stove in the dwelling-room was stoked from it, and the copper, and the bread oven, and in the open chimney itself the women stood cooking. The author visualises how the farmer's wife, during a pause in her work, sat here on a stool with a lump of brown sugar in

her mouth and a saucer of coffee balancing on three finger-tips as she gazed into the fire. Here people sat and talked, but he also called the open chimney a place of worry, where the thoughts of the woman rose with the eddying smoke.

But worries were not solely a woman's lot. The farmer also had grounds for worry – the running of the farm and how to pay his rent as a cypoholder when it fell due. There was indeed enough to turn over in their thoughts, sometimes no doubt the question of whether the buildings of the farmstead would remain standing.

No effort was made to conceal the wear of centuries when the Pebringe farmstead was re-erected at the museum. Perhaps by the very choice of this building, and the scrupulous attention to every detail of its dilapidation, a slightly exaggerated picture of the cowed Zealand peasant emerges. The miserable conditions of subsistence prior to the land reforms are clearly spelt out by the state of his farmstead. Nevertheless, such conclusions should not be drawn too hastily, for a building can well be crooked yet function as it should. And the crooked buildings of the Pebringe farmstead convey very relevantly something about the life of half-timbered buildings and their hardwearing qualities.

The durability of their construction is clearly felt just by looking at the wings of this farmstead. The timberwork has hung together for centuries. The most im-

In the farmstead from Pebringe the farmer sat at the head of the table, while the other men of the household sat with their backs to the window. The room was also used for sleeping in. Milk pans can be seen on the shelf nearest the kitchen.

Previous page: The only chimney in the Pebringe farmstead is the open chimney in the kitchen. Cooking was done on the raised hearth and the stove in the dwelling-room was stoked through the wall from the kitchen fire.

portant prerequisite for this was to keep the roof from leaking so that the timbers never started to rot.

When a building is moved in the manner adopted here, all traces of the repairs carried out by the occupiers in the course of the years remain. It can be seen how an extra plank has been nailed up here and there to strengthen what was about to subside. Obviously details such as these bring the people who lived here a little closer to us, giving us some idea of their daily problems. On the other hand, by straightening the wall timbers a large slice of the latter day history of the farmstead would be eliminated – additions and repairs disappear. However, traces showing that they had in fact been carried out are difficult to remove, and the timberwork would never quite regain its condition prior to the dilapidations.

A discussion of the removal technique used for the Pebringe farmstead must necessarily be extended to include some technical problems which are of great significance to the work of Frilandsmuseet. Since the farmstead was dismantled on its native site in 1938-39, and after it was opened at the museum in 1945, a slightly more moderate approach to these questions has taken shape. For example, it is now considered unacceptable from a pedagogical point of view that the Pebringe farmstead, with the interesting open chimney

it possesses, should be re-erected without a bread oven simply because this happened to have disappeared before the museum came on the scene. Nowadays, such extremes would not be gone to in order to reproduce exactly what has been found.

This leads us directly to the question of what the Pebringe farmstead should represent (and also for that matter the other buildings in the museum). Is it the individual farmstead which has to be re-created down to the last detail, so we experience it as time has handed it down to us? Or should the museum emphasise what is representative when re-creating the farmstead, and what was once usual in the region in question? To this we may answer that the museum has, since the beginning, endeavoured to find a suitable balance between the two extremes. The farmstead is first and foremost representative, i.e. an expression of a general custom. But it cannot be denied that it is the little individual details which help to make the buildings true to life.

The small oddities of the Pebringe farmstead should be seen in this light; for example, the way repairs have been carried out by successive generations. Yet it is common that country folk in the past managed in this way, and common for half-timbered buildings like living organisms to grow a little here, shrink a little there.

In countless farmsteads in Zealand part of the dwelling-house is older than the rest, and one can see that it has been added to at one time or another. The addition is often an "upper room" as in the Pebringe dwelling-house, neither is it unusual for a very old farmstead to have a wing added to it as late as the close of the 18th century.

It is primarily the period after these structural alterations which the Pebringe farmstead represents. Its condition corresponds more or less to the period shortly after 1800, but the green paintwork in the dwelling-room is as late as 1836, part of it covers a panel which is considerably older. But the mixture of periods is also something which corresponds closely with reality, and of this room we are primarily justified in saying that it illustrates an interior arrangement, the main features of which are characteristic of a very large number of peasant rooms in the past.

Wheelwright's Cottage

In the middle of the Zealand village at Frilandsmuseet stands a long building without additional wings and with two chimneys. As it is commonly known, a characteristic of old rural buildings in Zealand is that all fires are, as far as possible, grouped about one chimney, thus the two chimneys tell us that this building contains two dwellings. It also partly explains why the building is so long. But

this has not always been the case, for when the cottage was examined for the first time it was established that there were several phases in its building history. This examination was carried out in 1944, when the systematic registration of old rural buildings in Denmark, undertaken by the National Museum, reached Kalvehave in South Zealand. The cottage found here was so well preserved, that it was acquired the same year by Frilandsmuseet where it was opened in 1960.

Two families lived in the wheelwright's cottage from Kalvehave. Behind the stone wall is a saw pit with a log waiting to be sawn. To the right is a shed for storing the sawn timber.

During the measuring and surveying prior to its removal, and during the dismantling process, it was discovered that some of the bays at each end had gradually been added to an older nucleus. This is very evident for example, in the end which is broader than the rest of the building, but some of the other bays are also later additions, despite the fact that most of the building is constructed in the same half-timbering technique with tie beams mortised through unusually thick oak uprights.

Fortunately, the evidence revealed by the building is not the sole source of information about its past, for records have survived which tell us about the cottage, its occupants, and conditions in Kalvehave in bygone days. By combining the various kinds of evidence we are able to conclude that it was built during the last

decades of the 18th century when some farmsteads in Kalvehave were pulled down.

The building of houses on the sites of former farmsteads was a fairly common occurrence during the period of the great land reforms. Sometimes the farmsteads were actually demolished, sometimes they were moved away from the village, leaving a site which could be used for other purposes. The new houses often had a little land attached to them – a step forward indeed. Although the smallholder in reality received such little land that he was compelled to have another means of livelihood besides, a trade or else to work on neighbouring farms. It was also quite customary for new buildings not to be "new" in the true sense of the word. They could be adapted from the wing of a farmstead left behind when the other buildings were removed from the village, or made from old building materials salvaged from a farmstead which had been either pulled down or moved.

Something in this fashion appears to be the background of the Kalvehave cottage at Frilandsmuseet. The thick oak uprights have originally been part of a farmstead in the village. A little cottage which then grew in size – originally it was probably not more than a dwelling-room and kitchen with a chimney in the middle. Some outhouse rooms were soon added to one end, and the other end was also extended. At a later date, the latter was turned into a dwelling for the former occupier. In any event, we know that as from 1835 there were two dwellings in the building. At one stage the small dwelling was rented out, but later the occupants of the two dwellings were once again related to each other.

Gable of the outhouse end of the Kalvehave cottage and little shed for storing timber etc., the gable of which is built of boulders and packed with seaweed at the top.

The wheelwright's workshop is full of special tools. In the centre foreground is a shaving horse. The wheelwright sat astride the bench and worked wood held in a vice at the other end. To the left is a hub cradle used when spokes were fitted to the hub of the wheel. To the right is the lathe's flywheel.

This was when the son of the house took over the small dwelling. He was a wheelwright and built a workshop – the broad end of the building – in 1869.

Certain circumstances in the years to follow, perhaps about 1880, provide the basis for the way the building is arranged inside at Frilandsmuseet. For when it was acquired there were still some members of the family who could remember its interior in those days. This provided a welcome supplement to what could be seen in the structural details, and to what had been found in documents. Another extremely significant stroke of good fortune being that it was possible to recover a large amount of the things which had been in the house. Some were still in their old position, others had passed to different relations and now returned to their original setting. All these circumstances have helped to give this cottage a particularly realistic quality.

The two households living in the building were not strangers to each other. As we have seen, father and son with their families each had their own end of the cottage, and the two dwellings show how both the older and younger generation arranged their homes. However, it is not only variations in the arrangement of the homes that can be seen here, but the trades of father and son are also elucidated in considerable detail – these are not only very characteristic of the occupational patterns of smallholders in the past generally, but also of the special crafts of that particular locality.

The early dwelling, in which the older generation lived, is the one nearest the outhouse end of the building. It is entered either by the kitchen, or through the en-

In the oldest end of the wheelwright's cottage the table in the dwelling-room stands along the partition wall following old tradition. The small cabinet where the occupant kept his papers and articles of value is in its usual position in the corner on the bench. The "best room" can be glimpsed with a green cupboard for storing clothes and linen in. The shaving horse and a chopping block in the middle of the floor show that the room was also used as a workshop.

trance in the porch which leads into the dwelling-room. The small kitchen is almost entirely filled by the large open chimney, the floor space round it is minimal. It is a typical Zealand chimney – large enough to walk right into. Here the housewife stood when she had something on the hearth, and here, too, all the stoke holes to the other fires are gathered. The one for the stove in the dwelling-room is above the raised hearth in the chimney where the food was cooked. On the opposite side is the stoke hole for the copper, and in the rear wall of the chimney is the mouth of a bread oven, this oven is so large that it projects from the wall at the back of the house.

Just inside the dwelling-room, by the door, is the square iron stove which is quite enclosed and stoked from the hole in the chimney wall in the kitchen. This

type of stove so often encountered in old rural buildings in Denmark is of Norwegian origin. It must have been considered quite a valuable item in the modest home of a smallholder, but it was very essential if the dwelling-room were to be at all tolerable for living in during the cold winter months.

The family slept and ate in this room, and carried out a variety of indoor tasks here. The position of the table was probably considered a little old-fashioned because it stood in front of the partition wall, and not in front of the window as was usual in most homes in the locality, and in other regions virtually everywhere.

Through the other door of the dwelling-room can be glimpsed the "best room" used normally for storing linen and clothes, hence the chest and cupboard. But in this case, the room was also used by the smallholder as a workshop.

Here, then, we can round off our impression of how a smallholder subsisted. His livelihood was of course based on the smallholding, but the humble little barn and shed reveal all too clearly its limitations. A certain degree of specialisation was characteristic of the district around Kalvehave. Fruit-growing, for example, had played an important role for a long time, and the cottage has a fruit drying rack in the chimney. The workshop in the "best room" illustrates how a living was eked out besides; here are tools as well as a number of half-finished articles in a random mixture – all of wood.

This is again characteristic of the area. The extensive oak forests in the southernmost districts of Zealand had been maintained according to fairly advanced methods of forestry since the 1700's. For example, a deliberate effort was made to exploit the underwood, moreover apples and hops were cultivated in the forests. Special endeavours were made to increase the stand of hazel, used in the widespread barrel hoop industry. The smallholder who lived in the museum's cottage was actually called "hoop-maker", although he made other items, and concentrated particularly in his old age on wooden rakes, scythe handles, baskets, wooden spoons etc. In other words, he was an all-round craftsman who could turn his hand to almost anything.

The son, who lived in the other end of the building, was also a versatile craftsman. He had made, for example, the furniture of his little home beside the workshop he had himself added to the building. He could also cooper barrels, tan skins, make harvesting implements and offer his services in the neighbourhood as a glazier. Like his father, he also managed to fit in an extra means of livelihood as a fisherman. His primary trade, however, was that of wheelwright at which he had served his apprenticeship, and it is this that has left its mark on the workshop. Wagon wheels were made here on the lathe and felloe horse and assembled on the hub cradle. But before he reached this stage a supply of wood had to be sawn up and stored. Tree trunks were sawn into planks in the pit just outside the door of the workshop. Two men worked the pit saw, one man standing on top of the trunk and the other in the pit. The planks were stored for several years in the little detached shed before being brought into the workshop.

Opposite page: The weaver's cottage is built into the side of a hill and its back wall is fairly low. The bread oven protrudes from it.

Weaver's Cottage

The little whitewashed cottage with a thatched roof, huddled against the slope at the edge of the Zealand village at Frilandsmuseet, is the weaver's cottage from Tystrup in South-West Zealand. It was acquired in 1950 and opened in 1958.

Before paying a visit to the weaver and his family to see how they have arranged their home, we ought to look at the cottage more closely outside. For it is a type which was once extraordinarily widespread throughout the villages of Zealand, serving as a dwelling for the more humble class of country folk.

Most of the cottages like this have long since disappeared, and those which have survived are as a rule heavily modernised. And although it is possible to find a number of old-fashioned features in them here and there, it is unusual nowadays for them to be as unchanged as the cottage from Tystrup. A prerequisite for this is that the occupiers had not made any alterations for several generations.

The whole atmosphere of the exterior has remained unchanged. The characteristic whitewashed half-timbering of Zealand, for example, and another old Zealand custom: the coiled straw gable away from the road has not suffered the usual fate of gables of this kind which were sooner or later boarded up.

A straw gable is made of coils of straw pressed down between a close-set framework of sticks. The gable in the opposite end of the cottage is also interesting, particularly because it has a lean-to roof over two small sheds for pigs and chickens.

Previous page: The gables of the weaver's cottage are interesting. One is made of coiled straw pressed between sticks, while the other shown here has a lean-to roof over two small sheds for pigs and chickens.

Right: Most of the livestock in the museum roams free, but the spotted pigs are kept in a pigsty.

In the past more livestock could be kept as there had been a small outbuilding with standings for two cows, a little barn space, threshing floor and a fuel bunker. In its present form, however, the cottage has the appearance of being without land, whereas the occupant's trade as weaver provided the major means of support for his family. This is very striking once inside the cottage because the dwelling-room is dominated by a loom.

Before going into the dwelling-room one passes first into a little hall, which is actually part of the kitchen with an open chimney. Like the chimneys of other old buildings in Zealand, it is not solely a brick flue for smoke to pass through – its sheer size is noteworthy. As broad below as the room itself, it can be walked right into through the open front, and the floor of the room continues uninterrupted to the back of the chimney. Here, the person cooking could stand as the hearth does not entirely fill the chimney.

Food was cooked on the raised open hearth built of boulders collected from the fields. The fire simply burnt on the top of

this. The most important practical question, when using a hearth of this kind, is how to put the pots and pans over the fire. There had to be room for fuel, and cooking vessels had to be sufficiently raised above the fire to prevent them from putting it out. In addition, with air beneath them the bottom of the pots were heated and not just the sides. Sometimes pots and pans had legs high enough for them to stand over the fire. A gridiron for frying fish and sausages could be put on the embers. It was otherwise usual to raise cooking vessels over the fire by means of a trivet, or often – as in this cottage – a horizontal bar was also fitted into the chimney from which a kettle or pot could hang. A widespread method was by means of an adjustable ratchet hanger. This practical implement consists of two iron rods with ratchet teeth that adjust in relation to each other according to the length required.

The other fireplaces in the cottage are connected to this chimney. The stoke hole for the copper is at the bottom on one side, and at the rear of the chimney is the mouth of the bread oven that protrudes from the outside wall. It is a curiously low wall because the cottage is partially built into the slope. In the third wall of the chimney is the stoke hole for the stove in the dwelling-room.

The stove kept the room warm during the winter, and although the weaver probably kept warm enough while working at the loom, the rest of the family was undoubtedly glad of the warmth of the stove. It is therefore not surprising that the only armchair in the cottage stands here, as well as the baby's chair on the other side of the stove.

The mixed functions of this room is normal. The family ate at the table by the back window. The main sleeping place was in the large bed in the corner. The bench just inside the door could be used for a child to sleep on. There is also an extra bed in the little room behind the dwelling-room, and here too are a chest and cupboard for storing linen and clothing. A chest of drawers stands in the dwelling-room behind the loom, but the latter entirely dominates the interior. Generally, one of the most important functions of the dwelling-room is the variety of indoor tasks carried out in it; a special characteristic of this particular interior, though, is the extent to which the trade of the occupant overshadows it.

On the other side of the little hall-kitchen – the nucleus of this little house – is a room used partly as a scullery, partly as a kitchen, because the real kitchen virtually consisted of the open chimney with little space for much else. At the very end of the building is a room which was used as a workshop. Two details should be noticed here: firstly the clogmaker's tools, for clogmaking, like weaving, was often a craft in which smallholders specialised. In this case, the tools are a relic from the time there were clogmakers in the family before the two generations of weavers. The second interesting detail is the warping mill set aside in the workshop. The warping mill is a large rotating double frame upon which wool is wound before work on the loom begins. It is the means by which the wool is transferred to the loom when the warp is being put up between the loom's beams.

The Tystrup weaver, seen in a wider social and historical perspective, belonged to the borderline category between the cottage industry of the smallholder and the professional craftsman. It is clear, though, that the weaving done here was something entirely different to the weaving carried out in many cottages, and often in farmsteads. Other buildings in the museum contain looms, but this is because the woman of the house – sometimes a daughter or servant girl – wove cloth. Home weaving like that was not usual in Zealand, cloth was ordered from a real weaver such as the occupant of the Tystrup cottage.

As early as 1683 the Danish Law of that year decreed that weavers were among those craftsmen with permission to work in the countryside, whereas other trades had to keep to market towns. The rights of the country weaver were extended in 1737, after which weavers played an increasingly important role, and during the first half of the 19th century they steadily increased in numbers in the vil-

The weaver's loom fills the living-room of his cottage. When indoors the rest of the family gathered here. An accompaniment to their activities was the regular thump of the loom.

lages. In the vicinity of towns they often wove for unknown customers, and were a link in a capitalistic chain of production. But the typical village weaver, like the occupant of the Tystrup cottage, wove fabric for the women of the neighbourhood. When weaving was begun, the farmer drove his wife to the weaver. She brought yarn which had been spun on the farm, and often helped the weaver to set the loom. She could indicate the familiar striped patterns by winding the yarn in stripes round a stick or spool. The farmer and his wife usually brought various provisions with them when they drove to the weaver, for these were a major part of his payment.

Farm Labourer's Cottage From Englerup

There are two places called Englerup in Zealand, and this cottage comes from the one in Voldborg *herred*, west of Roskilde. It belonged to the Ryegård estate where the tenant worked.

The cottage was donated to the museum in 1946 and opened to the public in 1951 to mark the 50th anniversary of Frilandsmuseet's re-opening in Sorgenfri. Another little building from the same district, the fire station from Kirke Såby, was re-erected at the same time in close proximity once more to the Englerup cottage.

When Frilandsmuseet decides to move a building, it is only after many factors have been considered. A building must be truly representative of its kind at the museum, and fulfil one of the requirements in its general plan of acquisitions. These criteria also applied to the cottage from Englerup.

The intention in this case was primarily to illustrate how a farm labourer on an estate lived. But it is only one example, other homes of this kind have of course looked entirely different. The cottage is also intended to show something of the building traditions of the area. On both these points a deeper understanding can be gained of what this house has to tell, by comparing it with the other old buildings which are its neighbours.

First of all, it is very much a Zealand building in appearance, with its whitewashed walls and whitewashed half-timbering. This is very evident if we compare it with buildings from other parts of the country. However the Englerup cottage, seen in context with the other buildings from Zealand, reveals a number of different details which are characteristic of its native locality.

The half-timbering, for example, is worth studying more closely, as one will soon discover that two different methods have been adopted for mortising the timbers. In one method the timbers are mortised with tenons, i.e. the end of one piece of timber is fashioned to fit a hole in the other piece. This is in fact the normal method, and can be found in all the other half-timbered buildings in the museum. But in the cottage from Englerup a second method is also used whereby the end of one piece of timber is mortised into the side of another. It can be found in several parts of the house, for example where beams are mortised into upright posts in the outside walls below the wall plate, and in some cases in the middle of the uprights where horizontal timbers brace them in the walls.

But why did the joiner work in this rather haphazard fashion when he built the house, chopping and changing from one method to the other? In order to answer this question, the circumstances have to be considered in which the cottage came into being, although we know rather little about these. Possibly several men took part in building it, and each may have worked according to his own fashion. It is also possible that it was built round an older building – an abandoned farm building for example – and that this had to be repaired and added to. The general background, however, explaining why two different methods of mortising could occur in the cottage from Englerup is fairly widely known, that is to say, the locality is in the transitional zone between two areas of Zealand which each had its own joinery technique. In the northerly area the side mortise predominated, and in the southerly area the tenon technique.

Opposite page: The outshots typify the Englerup cottage. The one at the gable is for sheep.

A detail of this kind in the structure of a building, easily overlooked at a casual glance, is therefore able to provide the basis for many reflections on the building traditions of Zealand in general. Other features of the cottage are found in numerous Zealand buildings. The reed-covered outer walls, for example, can be seen in cottages which are neighbours at the museum. The reeds serve to insulate the walls, and prevent driving rain and rain coming from the thatching from washing away the clay from the wattle and daub walls. The seaweed along the ridge of the roof, on the other hand, is an entirely local phenomenon. Obviously presupposing that the locality is not far from a beach from which seaweed could be gathered. Englerup is situated by the inner reaches of Isefjord, therefore in this area seaweed

was not only used to cover ridges but sometimes as an in-filling for gables, as well as for banks and manure.

It is also interesting to compare the interior of the cottage with those of the other buildings which constitute the Zealand village. Opposite the Englerup cottage, on the other side of the village street, is the Pebringe farmstead for example. When one crosses the street from one building to the other, one must have a clear idea of what one is trying to compare, for it is not only the social difference between a farmer and farm labourer but also different periods. Therefore a true comparison is difficult to make.

The farm labourer appears to have had a dwelling-room which was as well equipped as that of the farmer. But this impression hinges on the fact that the Pebringe farmstead is arranged inside to correspond with the period about 1800, while the cottage from Englerup has an interior which dates from about 1900. There is thus a difference of a hundred years between them, a period of considerable development in so far as the arrangement of interiors is concerned. Moreover, the Englerup cottage is the first building to be re-erected at the museum whose interior is so recent, although the building itself is considerably older.

The reason for the late interior being that the widow and children of the last occupant donated virtually every piece of furniture etc. in the dwelling-room to Frilandsmuseet. The furniture stems from the marriage of his parents in 1884, although the paintwork we see now with imitation graining dates from 1910. It is also known that the armchair and firewood box was made by an old carpenter in Englerup c. 1900.

The purchase of the firewood box at this particular time is no coincidence, for a radical modernisation of the interior was undertaken at that period – the result of which we now see at the museum. The large iron stove with cooking ring was built into the dwelling-room, and it was this which necessitated the firewood box. It superseded an old-fashioned stove fired from a stoke hole in the open chimney. Another great improvement was made during these alterations when floor boards replaced the old clay floor.

It is therefore a constant disappointment to those who expect a setting of social misery, when visiting the home of a farm labourer on an estate, not to find it. The cottage is an example of the tolerable existence which could be led by settled, permanently employed farm workers, in spite of the fact that they belonged to the most poorly paid of the population. Neither is there evidence of serious friction between employer and employee, indeed to the contrary, a picture of the landowner on the wall would seem to indicate a bond of loyalty often encountered in patriarchal relationships.

Therefore, the farm labourer's cottage at Frilandsmuseet can be said to represent one end of a scale with many variations. The other end is not unfortunately represented. This is because the worst types of dwelling will not normally have survived and, in addition, they would be very difficult to re-create at the museum. We must suffice by imagining what it was like for seasonal farm labourers to live temporarily on an estate.

Fire Station and Village Pump

One of the advantages of community life in a village in the old days was its mutual fire fighting arrangements. In a densely built-up village fire represented a deadly risk, preventive measures were obviously of primary importance. Rules therefore

Above: The village fire engine outside the fire station. When the fire engine had to be used, the two wooden handles on top of the barrel were fitted into the holders for them at each end of the pump rod, and then pumping could begin.

Left: Competitions are held here during the autumn half-term. They are fun and informative.

118

existed stipulating the uses of fire, and chimneys were regularly inspected. If fire had already struck, devastating one or more farmsteads, it was only by mutual help that homeless families could be given shelter and their farmsteads rebuilt within a reasonable span of time. This was particularly the case prior to 1792, because from that date it was possible to take out a fire insurance policy covering rural buildings.

The only effective protection of buildings in the case of fire, apart from the direction of the wind, was a close-knit collaboration between as many people as possible in order to prevent – if they were lucky – the conflagration from spreading. Fire fighting aids were modest in the past, and although buckets of water could be quickly passed from hand to hand, a fire engine was far better. Machines of this kind have existed for almost 300 years, however it was not until much later that they became widespread. In Denmark a decree from 1764 laid down that every village in the country should have a fire engine with accessories. Many more regulations concerning fire brigades, village ponds (water supply for fire fighting) etc. followed later.

Therefore, a fire station is a characteristic feature among the buildings of a village. The fire station at Frilandsmuseet was put up in 1951 from Kirke Såby in Voldborg *herred,* west of Roskilde. It dates from about the middle of the 19th century, although its fire engine bears the date 1896, and is thus somewhat later.

The village pump close by is also presumably 19th century, the wooden pump – made from a hollowed out trunk – did not become common in the countryside

until the 19th century, and it was displaced at the close of the century by the iron pump. The hand pump in the museum's Zealand village has been the village pump in Pebringe. It has two spouts in order to enable a barrel on a wagon to be filled, e.g. the fire engine barrel had to be filled in this way. Before the advent of wells with hand pumps the only means of filling a fire engine was the village pond.

The hand pump from Pebringe could be used by all the inhabitants of the village, as not everybody had their own well. Indeed, until almost the end of the last century some of the villagers collected water from a water-hole. And even those who had a well perhaps preferred the village pump, which drew water from a greater depth and did not run dry in the summer months.

Village pump from Pebringe used by all the villagers. It is made of a hollowed out log with iron fittings.

Post Mill From Zealand

This mill was acquired in 1921 in Karlstrup near Køge, and has stood in the corner of the museum by Kongevejen since 1922. Familiar to passing traffic on this busy main road, it has become a landmark of Frilandsmuseet.

During the course of years hundreds of thousands of people have seen the mill and gained pleasure from it. Whereas if it had remained on its original site in Karlstrup, it would probably have disappeared by now like most of the other post mills which were once so numerous in Denmark.

The post mill was the usual type of windmill in this country until the so-called Dutch windmill supplanted it. This explains why post mills have not been built for so long in Denmark. The museum's post mill is also of venerable age, although the harnessing of wind power for milling

grain is far older. The earliest mention of a windmill in this country dates from the 1200's, characteristically enough from the Hedebo region where the Karlstrup mill comes from – a fertile plain in East Zealand unsuitable for watermills.

The post mill at Frilandsmuseet was mentioned in 1662 because it had been rebuilt after having burnt down during the Swedish War. Much of the mill, however, was reconstructed in the 1700's. The most long lasting component of a mill of this kind is the post itself, sheltered beneath and within the mill which can be turned according to the direction of the wind. The big vertical post has given mills of this type their name.

Smallholder's Farmstead From Tågense

The relationship between this cottage and visitors to the museum is slightly curious. Some guests almost wear it threadbare with interest while others walk past it unheedingly. This is due to its position in the corner of the museum close to Kongevejen. If one turns left after going through the main entrance it is the first house to visit, but if one turns right it is normally the last building in the museum. And there is a great difference in the energy of visitors at the outset and conclusion of a tour of the museum. Particularly if they have not followed the advice given in the guide to select a few buildings to see more closely on a single visit.

The cottage was situated in a corner in the past, too, as Tågense is a village in the most south-easterly corner of the island of Lolland. It was acquired here in 1928 and removed in 1936, but not opened at the museum until 1946.

Whether seen first or last, it is one of the buildings at the museum which relates a little about the daily life of humble folk in bygone days throughout the countryside, although its occupants were not among those who lived in the greatest poverty, for they at least had a cottage which provided the mainstay of their existence. The five acres attached to it were not enough to live off, though, and the smallholder had to work as a day labourer on neighbouring farms.

Like most of the homesteads in the museum, the impression it gives varies

according to when it is seen. On a fine sunny day it seems idyllic, especially if it has been freshly whitewashed. Indeed, many who visit it on a day like this, feeling the current nostalgia for old rustic dwellings, would be prepared to move in, at any rate for a short time during the summer. But the atmosphere is slightly different on a wet gloomy winter's day, when perhaps the whitewashed walls are peeling and damp patches of clay can be seen in the walls. Most people would then think twice before moving in, for in these conditions it is not hard to perceive that to live in this cottage day in day out, year after year, is an existence far removed from ours today.

The everyday life of the occupants of this cottage was not basically any different to that of the other families who have lived in the other homes now at the museum. Farmer and smallholder lived in very similar conditions: both homes were separated from the soil at floor level only by a layer of stamped clay, both homes normally had only one room which could be heated, and in which most indoor tasks were carried out during the winter months. Both farmstead and smallholding were virtually self-supporting.

The social difference between farmer and smallholder was not presumably more noticeable until well into the latter half of the 19th century when the farming community underwent certain changes. These were felt by the smallholder when he worked as a day labourer. He had his meals provided by the farm on which he worked almost the entire day, but during this period more and more farms had a servants' hall where workers on the farm

had their meals – the smallholder working as a day labourer was no longer part of the family to the same extent as earlier. And in addition, the gap between farmer and smallholder widened apace with the increasing social influence of the farmer in general. It was not until the turn of the century and the introduction of State smallholdings that conditions began to improve for the smallholder. This social difference left its mark, too, on their homes, for whereas technical improvements found their way to many a farm, the smallholder could not afford to make changes.

Therefore the farmsteads of smallholders often retain structural features viewed somewhat unfeelingly by experts from museums as excitingly old-fashioned and primitive. Some constructions in the Tågense cottage, for example, are undoubtedly alike those used an extremely long time ago. Indeed, the term "prehistoric" to describe some structural details found in it is almost certainly justified, although nowadays the majority of people would be more likely to consider the use of the word "prehistoric" to symptomise a certain evolutionary trend of thought akin to that of Bernhard Olsen in the past.

One of the primitive constructions are the Y-shaped uprights carrying the roof of the western outshot. In small unpretentious buildings naturally forked branches like these were often used in the old days. It was a simply executed method – another piece of timber could rest in the forks and no carpenter was required for complicated mortises. This explanation has always appealed to scholars of rural building constructions. However, the background of this type of casual felling need not have its roots in antiquity. There is possibly a more prosaic explanation such as a lack of building skill on the part of the smallholder, or perhaps it was easier to collect broken branches than building timber in the woods of the estate.

Previous page: The Tågense cottage as seen from the post mill with the other farmstead from the island of Lolland in the background. The nearest gable end forms an outshot built of boulders with a sloping roof. A pig was once kept here, and behind the sty was a small fuel bunker.

123

The dwelling-room in the Tågense cottage was used for sleeping, eating and working in as can be seen from bed, table and spinning-wheel. It was heated by a stove stoked from the open chimney in the kitchen, and clothes could be dried above the stove.

The outshot of the west gable is curious for another reason as well: the walls are built of granite boulders bonded like stone walling. The foremost room had a pigsty and behind this was a fuel bunker. In the same end of the cottage was a barn with a stall for a cow or two, and after this a threshing-floor. From the threshing-floor and the pantry beside it can be seen some narrow rooms along the back of the house.

These narrow rooms are a so-called outshot, and they are the result of a special building tradition fairly frequently encountered in old houses on Lolland. An outshot of this kind is a narrow low extension from the nave of the building, the roof projects over it from the inner roof-bearing walls to the low outer walls of the outshot about a metre from the inner walls. Thus a number of narrow rooms between the two walls can be arranged beneath the eaves of the roof. These rooms were largely used for stores. For example, in the Tågense farmstead the room in the outshot by the threshing-floor was used as a chaff shed, i.e. chaff from the threshing-floor was stored here and used as fodder for livestock. The room by the pantry is a larder where salted or cured meat and preserves were stored, in Danish it is called *sulekammer, sule* being preserved pork, from which we may construe that the pig in the pigsty ended its days here.

The position of the furniture in the dwelling-room has, as usual, been decided by the sources of heat and light. The table is obviously not placed by the windowless northern wall even though this is nearer the stove, instead it is beneath the windows, and the seating arrangement is a movable bench along the wall. The absence of a bench on the other side of the table away from the wall is no accident, because Lolland was one of the regions where it was not customary for the women of the house to sit at table for meals – they simply carried the food in and out. This custom was not so marked among smallholders and there were no doubt exceptions, for the smallholder had no outside help such as servants whose presence on farms probably helped to uphold the custom.

This room was also the sleeping place for the family – in the corner opposite the table is a four-poster bed decorated with a painted floral motif that is characteristic of folk art in Lolland. There is also sleeping accommodation in the "best room" on the other side of the little kitchen with its large open chimney. The "best room", like the workshop in the gable, is a later addition, and a chest and chest of drawers in it were used for storing clothing and linen. In this particular farmstead the "best room" was also used for indoor jobs. The loom stands here, and in the middle of the room is the warping mill from which the yarn is transferred to the loom when the warp (the longitudinal threads) is put up. During the winter months the regular thump of the loom being worked must have echoed through the cottage, for weaving was an important means of earning extra. Because weaving is fairly strenuous it could be carried out in an unheated room, moreover it is said that wool is best woven away from warmth.

The Dannemare Farmstead

The island of Lolland is represented at Frilandsmuseet by two smallholder farmsteads and a village meeting place where farmers sat on a circular platform of earth with a tree in the centre. In Denmark it is called a "village meeting tree". However, even though the meeting place lay right outside their doors, it is not certain whether smallholders took part in the meetings as in most places it was a right reserved for farmers.

The farmstead we see here is a smallholding, but there is a degree of difference between it and the Tågense smallholding.

The impression gained from the latter of the living conditions of the more humble countryfolk has been somewhat mitigated by the addition of the Dannemare farmstead in Frilandsmuseet. It comes from the westerly part of Lolland, in the district south of Nakskov. It was acquired in 1950 and opened at the museum in 1957.

When looking round the Dannemare farmstead one quickly gets the impression that the family who lived here managed a little better than the family in the other Lolland smallholding. The farmstead does not just stand in a field but is surrounded by a neat garden with flowers and vegetables. Once inside one is struck by the excellent housing conditions in view of the fact that this has been the home of a small-holder. It is quite spacious and both of the living-rooms have wooden floors. There is also a fairly modern stove in comparison with the stove in the Tågense home which was stoked from the open chimney.

This very evident discrepancy between the two farmsteads from the same island has both an economic background and a time factor to explain it. The occupants of the Dannemare farmstead had been able to buy their smallholding from their land-lord at a fairly early date, in addition to which it had a little more land than most other smallholdings and subsequently a better economy. And as far as the time factor is concerned, the interior of the Dannemare dwelling-house at the muse-um is almost a generation later than that from Tågense. Time had passed and pro-gress in general had enabled a few of the less privileged to better their position a little by dint of hard work and enterprise.

Nevertheless, although some details of the farmstead would have been consider-ed up-to-date by contemporary standards in the mid-19th century compared to many other homes, it certainly had other features which went way back in time. For example, one of the considerations which strongly influenced the selection of this farmstead for removal to the museum was a panelled room in which the table was placed along the partition wall.

Table and seating arrangements are something which experts note down energetically when inspecting old rural buildings. This is because it has long been realised that there are two forms of table arrangement which predominate in old Danish dwelling-rooms. In one, the table is beneath the windows, in the other it is along a partition wall. The former arran-gement is by far the most common, while the latter is more local and only found in certain areas, for example Lolland, Falster and South Zealand.

In the course of the 20th century most rural homes have been influenced by urban fashions, and the table is usually in the middle of the room surrounded by chairs. However, this re-arrangement has often taken place so recently that some people can remember where the table originally stood. By approaching old people for information it has proved pos-sible for ethnologists to establish that the custom of placing a table along a parti-tion wall also existed in parts of West Zealand and the island of Bornholm.

The reason why research on this subject has been followed with such interest, is not because it has any great significance as far as the daily life and indoor pastimes of the occupants are concerned, whether a table stood one way or the other. It is because the arrangement with a table

The carefully tended garden of the farmstead from Dannemare, Lolland, with flowers in front of the living-room windows and a kitchen garden with currant bushes and cabbages.

126

View towards the Dannemare farmstead from the Tågense cottage. The covered gateway between the two wings leads into the farmyard. The garden is enclosed by a wattle fence.

along a partition wall is considered to be a relic of a far earlier cultural stadium. It is a reminiscence of the times before a sweeping change in the interior of dwellings occurred – the introduction of windows to admit light earlier provided by the louver in the roof. The table placed against a partition wall is a relic of the Middle Ages before windows were generally adopted. It was not until then that there was any reason to move the table nearer the light. In some areas the new custom was not followed for quite a long time, although there is a record from Lolland of a glass window in a farmstead as early as 1505.

In this case, then, the position of the table is of interest, while its appearance is not. Furniture, though, is often interesting and should not be overlooked. In the kitchen of the Dannemare farmstead, for example, there is a cupboard table, more often called a chest table. This stands in front of the window, but it has probably been banished at some time or other from a more honoured position in one of the dwelling-rooms. It is an early type of furniture which has undoubtedly been widespread throughout Lolland as far back as the 18th century. Most of these pieces of furniture, however, have most likely either disappeared or been relegated to secondary rooms before the close of the 19th century.

The kitchen is in itself a curious mixture of old and new, with an old-fashioned open chimney but a bread oven – in this case small enough to be contained within the walls of the cottage – with an iron

127

The table in the living-room of the Dannemare farmstead is along the partition wall. The "best room" can be glimpsed beyond.

Previous page: The gable of the Dannemare farmstead is typical for the island of Lolland, but the sweep well is a very widespread type.

door. Sausages, pork etc. could be smoked in the open chimney, for this purpose a stand for hanging the meat on could be moved freely in and out of the chimney. It has hooks at the top from which foodstuffs for curing in this way were hung. Another method of smoking and storing is with the so-called bacon rack which hangs in the scullery beside the chimney. It is a block of wood with wooden pegs in for hanging the meat. The raised hearth of boulders in one side of the chimney is

also old-fashioned, for this left enough space for the person cooking to work right inside the chimney. Often an easier method has been adopted in more recent times as we see here, in that the stoke hole to the stove next door has disappeared. Its absence is explained by going into the dwelling-room which no longer has an extension stove but a stove that has to be stoked and fired independently. It has cooking rings, and could thus be used not only for keeping food warm but also for modest meals. The warmth and smell of food cooking issuing from this stove must have given the dwelling-room a tinge of life that is perhaps missed at the museum. The warmth from it, however, did not

reach the "best room" with its chests for storing linen and clothes, and in this case an extra bed.

Built in the form of a right-angle, the Dannemare farmstead has a threshing floor in continuation of the dwelling-house. On the other side of the covered gateway is the barn and cowsheds at right-angles. A strange feature are the small box-like compartments for sand, dogs and chickens. The pigsty has been in the little outshot jutting into the court-yard. The workshop is in the little separate building in the courtyard, and in it is a separate compartment for geese. After walking past the sweep well we come to the gable of the dwelling-house which is perhaps the most characteristic Lolland feature of the farmstead. It is a thatched gable which overhangs an earlier wattle gable, implements etc. could be stored beneath it, propped against the wall. A hay carrier hangs from the gable; this was a useful implement for bringing in hay if there were no horse, besides which it could be used if a meadow were too swampy for a horse and cart to drive across.

The Lundager Farmstead

The farmsteads and cottages from the island of Funen, closely grouped and in a village, were the first to give visitors to Frilandsmuseet an impression of something regionally complete. The affinity between the buildings is further emphasised by their position round a village green – common ground where all could meet –

Above: Edged with box the flower beds in the old-fashioned garden of the Dannemare farmstead are at their prettiest when the peonies are in full flower.

Below: Fuchsia bordering a garden path at the Lundager farmstead is a fine sight when in bloom.

A combination of stone walling and wattle fencing separates the pasture from the garden at the Lundager farmstead. To the right hop poles stick up.

for here is the meeting place: a ring of stones beneath a lime tree, the pond and the forge. All were part of the amenities available to every villager. The buildings from Funen were also the first to give an impression of the variations within the building traditions of a specific region. The reason for this is that the museum concentrated on Funen for a number of years during the Twenties and Thirties. The Lundager farmstead was the first and largest of the buildings to be acquired. It was bought in 1924, two wings were re-erected in 1926 but it was not entirely complete until 1934. The Lundager it comes from is in South-West Funen in the parish of Gamtofte close to the town of Assens.

Like most of the farmsteads and cottages at the museum it was once a copy-holding under an estate, and evidence of this is immediately seen on reaching the gate leading into the courtyard, as it bears a number plate, the number on which corresponds to the number of the farmstead in the register of the manor estate of Brahesborg's holdings. Another point to notice is the date 1830 by the gateway because it tells us something of significance about rural buildings in general. For after crossing the courtyard we then notice the date 1747 over the front door of the dwelling-house. This illustrates very clearly that the buildings of a farmstead are rarely built at the same time. Even the age of a single wing may differ, in that a given date may only apply to a single bay in the wing. This is also the case in the Lundager farmstead which is

131

In the covered gateway of the large, four winged Lundager farmstead can be seen details of a ridge post construction still to be found in a few old buildings in West Funen. The roof is primarily carried by ridge posts standing at intervals through the middle of the building beneath the ridge. The ridge post in the photograph is just inside the gateway. It is braced by struts from the tie beam. At the very top beneath the ridge is a strut for strengthening the structure from gable to gable. It joins the ridge post to the ridge beam.

supposed to have more building phases than those shown by the two dates.

Yet it would be a pity to be so engrossed by dating problems as to miss other details when entering the courtyard through the covered gateway. If one gazes upwards, the gateway has more to reveal, namely a roof construction which few can say they have at home. Otherwise most of the old buildings at the museum have a raftered roof which is in principle the same as that still found in most Danish houses today. But the construction to be seen in the gateway is different, its most important structural feature being the upright post in the middle of the building beneath the ridge which carries the roof. It is a so-called ridge post construction, and in Funen a structure with prehistoric origins. The ridge posts stand at intervals through the middle of the building and support the ridge beam, a pole lying horizontally under the ridge. The top ends of the rafters ride on the ridge beam without tie beams. Rafters riding like this are called "hanging trees" in Danish.

A visit to the Lundager farmstead reveals how much can be learned about a building before going any further than the gateway – just by using one's eyes. Once across the courtyard the same question arises as that when on a real country visit: which door to enter the house by? At the museum it does not matter, for all rooms can be seen but just in a different order. In the countryside, however, it does matter because there is a great difference between the two doors. One is the best entrance and not used daily. The other is the door to the scullery and the one normally used.

Opposite page: In the yellow light of the late afternoon the courtyard has a special atmosphere. There was once wood to be chopped here and people crossed to and fro on errands in the outbuildings.

The scullery is in many ways an intriguing room, particularly when it is not used simply as a passage room as so often the case. A great number of tasks can be carried out here. All rough chores, for example, especially those which need heat from a fire. The chimney in the scullery is a large open chimney with a number of stoke holes for other fires. Cooking, though, was not often done here. On this point there is a difference between the regions west of the Great Belt and Zealand to the east. Most old farmsteads in Funen have two chimneys: one for cooking which also heated the dwelling-room, the other in the scullery for everything else.

The very name in Danish *bryggers* indicates that beer was brewed here. The large quantity of warm water needed for this was brought to the boil in a built-in copper. The drying of malt also needs a fire. In the scullery chimney of the Lundager farmstead a malt kiln has been built into one of the chimney walls. Warmth and smoke from the chimney passed into the kiln through smoke holes, and the

malt was laid on a rack in the kiln. Water was boiled in the copper for other heavy household duties such as laundering and slaughtering. The scullery has no fewer than two bread ovens for baking, one large and one small. It was also used for butter and cheese making, under the ceiling are milk pans for skimming milk. The cider-press in the corner indicates what was earlier a speciality of Funen: cider. The orchard outside shows that the people of Funen took pride in their cider. Another of their specialities in the past was hop-growing, the flowers of which give beer its taste. In the garden in the summertime you will see hops growing up poles.

In the summer months, too, the hearth in the scullery was often used for cooking in Funen. In the winter, on the other hand, the hearth in the dwelling-room was used. Thus the room was kept cool in the summer and warm in the winter, when heat from the open chimney was the only means of keeping the room warm. It was, in the modern sense, a combined kitchen and living-room.

The chimney in the dwelling-room is an open chimney with a raised hearth filling the base of the chimney, with a compartment beneath it for fuel. The fire simply burned on the flat surface of the hearth and pots and kettles were placed over the fire by means of an iron trivet or hung from a chimney-crane consisting of a vertical iron bar in the side of the chimney, to which was attached a horizontal arm that could be swung out at various angles, in many cases its height was adjustable.

As we have seen, the room was used both as a kitchen and living-room, i.e. the family both ate and slept here, and

The room in the side wing of the Lundager dwelling-house is used for weaving in during the summer months. Today people can watch a demonstration of old-fashioned weaving here.

This was the room where the occupants of the Lundager farmstead lived. The farmer and his wife slept in the finely decorated alcove bed, and meals were eaten at the table chest.

probably gathered here when not busy elsewhere. And casual visitors were no doubt invited into this room for a chat.

The interior of the room has of course been influenced by this miscellany of functions. Cooking demanded not only a hearth, but a table, with dishes and bowls within reach, as well as a place for storing food. There is a larder in a little passage just outside, and in the room is a built-in food safe, and storage space in the bottom

of a dresser, and in a table chest. The dresser, plate rack and table chest could be used for storing kitchen utensils. The table chest with its useful cupboard-like base could be used either as a work table or eating table. And, when tidied up after meals, it was a presentable spot for the communal beer jug to stand, so that anybody coming in thirsty and tired could take a gulp from it.

Everything in the workshop of the Ørbæk forge is tidy. Every tool has its place be it hammer or pliers – regardless of size.

Forge From Ørbæk

The forge by the village pond is one of the impressions of a village idyll usually remembered by those who have visited the museum. The red-washed half-timbered building reflected in the water, and ducks swimming placidly on the reed encircled pond. The pollarded poplars at the water's edge are typical of many villages in Funen.

It is not surprising that the Ørbæk forge is one of the most photographed motifs at Frilandsmuseet. Its picture has been used on the covers of the museum guides for many years.

The position of the forge is by no means accidental, although it is not situated here solely to provide a charming setting for photographers – excellent though this intention may be. The museum is obviously aware of the attraction of idyllic old buildings and rural settings that draws many people to Frilandsmuseet. But once in the museum people will also profit from what is offered in addition to this: the realisation that conditions in which countryfolk lived in the past do not as a rule agree very well with the popular conception of a rustic idyll.

The reason why forges were often situated in the middle of villages is in many cases due to the special position of the blacksmith in the peasant community. The blacksmith was not an independent tradesman in the modern sense, he was appointed by the farmers and virtually an official of the village. He did not receive payment for each job, but instead was given a certain amount of farm produce each year from those for whom he worked. Therefore the blacksmith often lived in a cottage built on the village green – the common land in the heart of the village.

Frilandsmuseet has attempted to illustrate the usual setting of a forge in a village before the land reforms, although it is a little disturbing, and in a way a little curious, to know that the history of the forge at the museum is an entirely different one. True, it looks exactly like the village forges it is meant to represent, but its own background in fact reflects the local disputes of a period in which

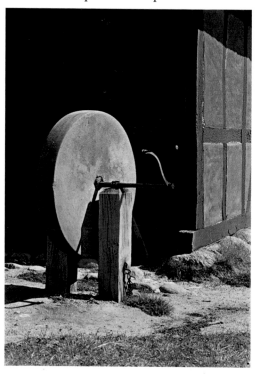

common village rights were in a state of dissolution. The group of people responsible for the building of the forge in 1846 had in fact broken away from the village fellowship centred round an older forge in Ørbæk. Thus the forge built in 1846 was acquired by the museum in 1934, and in the course of the next two years it was moved from its native village Ørbæk in East Funen and re-created at Sorgenfri.

The forge had not been in use for a number of years by the time it was acquired, therefore the tools of the blacksmith's trade had entirely disappeared. The tools to be seen today in the forge have been collected from other forges in Funen. On the other hand, the dwelling-rooms at the back of the cottage had been inhabited until shortly before the building was taken over by the museum. The last occupant was the daughter of the last blacksmith to work the forge, and she had not altered her childhood home much. The blacksmith before her father had been a bachelor, but her parents had seven children, and in order to gain more space the last blacksmith had added an alcove bed in the dwelling-room which projected into the woodshed.

The smith has spent most of his time in the forge in the front part of the cottage. The most important detail of its interior, as in all forges, is the hearth. It is built up like a raised open hearth in the bottom of an open chimney. But unlike a raised hearth for cooking in a kitchen, the fire had to have a far higher temperature. This was obtained by means of bellows beside the chimney. The blacksmith put the iron into the fire, and to make the iron red-hot he pumped the handle of bellows to fan air into the flames.

There is a grindstone outside the forge. Much of the blacksmith's work was done out of doors, such as shoeing horses.

Flax Kiln

This curious little construction stands in a thicket behind the buildings from Funen. This is the usual place for a flax kiln, as it was understandably considered to be a potential fire risk and therefore kept at some distance from thatched buildings. The flax kiln at the museum originally stood a little way behind a farmstead in Skovby, Bregninge parish on the island of Ærø, until it was taken down in 1962 and re-erected at the museum in 1966.

The kiln was used for drying flax. Flax being the raw material for linen caused it to be widely cultivated by peasants in the old days. The stalks from which the fibre is won have to undergo a series of processes before spinning. The flax has to be soaked and then dried, for example. The drying process was usually done in a simple earth pit with a fire. However, in some regions more elaborate methods were adopted. The flax kiln from Ærø represents a variation of the kilns used in the easterly districts of North Schles-

The flax kiln was stoked from the opening in the bottom, warm air then seeped up through the flax arranged on iron bars half-way up.

wig, Ærø and South Funen. These kilns presumably originated during the first half of the 19th century, when measures were taken to improve the cultivation of flax.

Smallholder's Farmstead From Årup

Most people who have travelled through Funen will have noticed the small half-timbered farmsteads built with three wings which are still to be found in fairly large numbers. They resemble the smallholder's farmstead from Årup in the heart of westerly Funen which Frilandsmuseet acquired in 1926, although it was not opened to the public on its new site until 1935. It is conspicuously situated here just by the village green and is very much part of the Funen setting.

The outward appearance of the cottage contributes to this impression. Not only its three wings, but also the way in which the half-timbering is kept in repair. In the tradition usual for Funen, the timbers are painted in a dark colour which sets off the pattern of the half-timbering in contrast to the whitewashed in-filling. One of the seasonal tasks carried out each year in the spring approaching Whitsuntide was to repair the outside walls, whitewash them and repaint the half-timbering. In Funen there seems to have been a tradition of punctiliousness on this point.

Neatness and care also appear characteristic of many cottage gardens in Funen. The Årup cottage has an old-fashioned garden, rather like that of the Lundager farmstead, divided into plots containing flowers and herbs. Hops, the speciality of

The dwelling-room in the Årup farmstead was heated by an iron stove which is self-contained with its own flue and not stoked from the kitchen.

Funen seen in both gardens, seem to have played a certain role too. The impression that they are not grown in such quantity simply for home brewing is confirmed if we look into the outbuilding. For here stands a hop press used for packing hops to be sent away for sale.

Over the front door of the dwelling-house is the date 1760 and an inscription. A lobby leads into the kitchen where members of the family mostly gathered when indoors. They could sit by the win-

Previous page: The windows of the Årup homestead are almost entirely hidden when the hollyhocks flower. Idyllic half-timbering and well tended gardens are often considered specially typical of Funen.

dow, and the open chimney warmed the room, although its primary function was for cooking. It is the type usual in westerly Denmark in the past, in that the raised fireplace completely fills the bottom of the chimney.

However, the kitchen is very small, consequently the dwelling-room beside it has been constantly used, also for sleeping in, as the cottage's two alcove beds are in here along the back wall. The heating of this room is quite interesting, for the iron stove is not like those stoked from the open chimney. It is self-contained with its own flue, and stoked directly through a door in its iron casing: a method which entailed carrying fuel into a room heated by a stove of this kind. The self-contained stove in the Årup cottage is one of the early types – often with the simple box shape of their predecessor, the extension stove stoked from the open chimney. It bears the date 1724 and, like most of the iron stoves used throughout the countryside in the 1700's, it has been imported from Norway.

There is also a "best room" which, true to custom, remained unheated and was primarily used for storing linen and clothing in the chest etc. standing there. In the western wing is a room for the old folk of the family, and in this case there is no kitchen attached to it, therefore the old couple must have eaten with the rest of the family. Normally, too, the older generation living like this was in close

touch with the younger members of the family in the home, helping with light chores as strength permitted; for example small jobs about the house, building repairs, and the care of grandchildren. Moreover, the kitchen provided the old folk with warmth, for all they had otherwise was a bed wagon – a transportable semi-cylindrical framework for holding a container of embers – with which they could warm the bed in their own room.

Clogmaker's Cottage

Seen at a distance, this cottage can well lead us to believe that we have been misinformed. For here is a completely whitewashed building, whereas we have just read that the normal custom for Funen is the accentuation of half-timbering by painting it. This general rule is indeed correct but there are also exceptions to it. Some districts in East Jutland likewise follow an old custom of whitewashing half-timbering, this is also the case in Funen although as we have seen, it is primarily characteristic of Zealand. The choice of colour may also vary. In Funen the usual combination is whitewashed infillings between dark timbers, but here and there a redwash, or particularly a yellow, is preferred. However, once in the courtyard of the clogmaker's cottage we can see that the occupants have reverted to the normal custom of painting the half-timbering, in this case the façade of the dwelling-house.

To be able to mention a courtyard in connection with such a relatively little building may seem curious, but it is not a special feature of this cottage alone. Here, too, the museum has acquired a building which is representative of a type formerly found in considerable numbers. The cottage was acquired in 1936. Its native site is the village of Kirke-Søby, South-West Funen. It was moved to Frilandsmuseet where it was opened in 1939. Like the cottage from Årup, there is still quite a number of cottages in Funen which resemble the Kirke-Søby homestead in lay-out. Indeed, they often look like the smallholding from Årup but with a narrow additional wing shutting off the courtyard from the road. In this way, all the obvious advantages of an enclosed courtyard were obtained: a pleasant spot for chopping kindling, mending and sharpening implements, etc. Prestige reasons, however, should not be overlooked in considering the preference in Funen for buildings with four wings. It is very possible that a smallholder simply wanted to emulate the home of a farmer. Neither can we reckon as a matter of course that the number of wings to a building cor-

Behind the hedge is the clogmaker's little garden with neat flower beds in geometrical patterns. The façade of the cottage is completely whitewashed which is somewhat unusual in Funen. To the right the bread oven juts out from the wall under a lean-to.

Opposite page: The west side of the clogmaker's cottage is particularly charming when sunlight accentuates its mellow surface. The fold in the foreground is fenced in with wattles, here sheep shelter from the sun beneath a chestnut tree.

responds to the amount of land farmed.

The Kirke-Søby cottage has had little land attached to it. This can be felt as soon as we see the modest barn and pens for livestock, but as is so often the case, the occupant did not solely subsist by farming. It was normal for smallholders to be engaged in some form of cottage industry. Not, in the present context, the various crafts which were widespread among countryfolk prior to industrialisation in a society based largely on a subsistence economy. But smallholders sometimes specialised in a particular trade or craft and sold their products retail. This kind of specialisation is an important feature of the occupational background of the Kirke-Søby cottage. And when an occupational characteristic has to be illustrated in an open-air museum, it is very fortunate when such a specialisation is clearly manifested by the interior of a building or the utilisation of its rooms, as can be seen here in the wing containing the workshop of the clogmaker.

Even before going into the workshop we are aware of the kind of trade carried on within. The beech logs by the wayside

The clogmaker's cottage from Kirke-Søby, South-West Funen, is very small and strangely enough for a building of this size it is quadrangular in shape with a courtyard in the middle. Passing through the covered gateway into the little yard we see that the façade of the dwelling has dark half-timbering in the Funen tradition.

indicate woodwork of some sort, and the clogmaker's sign by the covered gateway removes the last vestige of doubt. Once inside the workshop we can follow the different stages of clogmaking – from a wooden block of suitable size to the finished clog. One of the most important implements in the workshop is the shaving horse. Here the clogmaker sat astride the bench (hence the name horse), and with his feet pressed a treadle which by lever action grips the work in a vice at one end of the bench. It was a fixture in the workshop of a clogmaker, but it was also to be found in the workshop of many another handy smallholder.

The clogmaker's workshop is in the wing which had earlier been the dwelling-

The workshop of the clogmaker is in the wing formerly the dwelling-house. The clogmaker had little land, and spent most of his time in the workshop, particularly in the winter when no farming could be done. His customers visited him in his workshop if they bought new clogs or to be measured for a pair to be made. On the chopping block to the left is a piece of wood for making into a clog – it looks very like a piece of firewood. Beech was often used, but alder and other light woods were also suitable. The axe by the chopping block was used for the first rough dressing. On the shaving horse in the middle of the room and elsewhere in the workshop are clogs in various stages of production. Lasts are ranged on a shelf and finished clogs along the beam.

146

house. The latter had been superseded by the present dwelling-house which is a little broader and higher, but by no means a large dwelling. In the true Funen tradition, it has nevertheless two chimneys – something which would have been virtually unthinkable in Zealand. One of the chimneys belongs to the scullery, and the large bread oven projecting from the outside wall on the garden side was stoked from it. The other open fireplace is in the combined kitchen and living-room. Warmth was provided by the raised open hearth, where the cooking was done. This room also has two alcove beds, but there is an additional alcove bed in the "best room" which was otherwise furnished with storage furniture.

Watermill From Funen

A sunken road is reached after a few minutes if one walks a little further into the museum from the Funen buildings. It cuts gradually deeper and deeper into the terrain to end finally in front of a large half-timbered house at the bottom of a valley – it is the watermill from Funen.

Its position is a typical one for a large watermill. Moreover, the museum had the good fortune to find a site in the park that corresponds very closely to the original locality. Until 1949 this was in the parish of Ellested in East Funen, close to Ørbæk between the towns of Nyborg and Ringe. It was known as Nymølle, and beside the same stream there was a Gamlemølle (New Mill and Old Mill). Both mills were under the manor of Lykkesholm close by. Nymølle was reached by a sunken road that cut its way down the side of a valley, and the miller's garden stretched from the road, and along the foot of the hill over to the mill pond. When the mill was dismantled, the museum not only measured and surveyed the buildings but also the garden. It has therefore been possible to re-create the setting more or less as it was originally, with two linden trees on each side of the garden gate, the same ferns along the garden path, the broad leaved *polygonum* at the bottom of the slope, and a round summer-house with a discarded millstone to serve as a table.

A walk round the garden gives an idea of the lay-out of the watermill: a long dwelling-house which also contains the mill in one end, and a transverse wing towards the garden containing the scullery. Although the watermill could be opened to the public in 1964, it was not until 1972 before the museum could begin the first practical preparations for re-erecting the outbuildings.

In its entirety the watermill comprises four wings. The dwelling-house is detached but the remaining three wings are adjoining, and they contain barns, stables, cowshed and other outhouse accommodation necessary for the farming carried out by the miller in conjunction with the running of the mill.

The reason why the watermill was not fully re-erected all at once is because Frilandsmuseet did not originally own the plot on which the outbuildings could be put up. However, there was no doubt that the position chosen for the watermill, just by the museum boundary, was the right one, therefore everyone had to reconcile themselves to the fact that it would have to be re-erected in several stages. The terrain could be adapted without undue difficulty, and it would be possible to create a mill pond by borrowing water from Mølleåen, the river flowing past in the valley. By this means a sufficient supply of water would be ensured to work the mill.

Today, visitors to the museum can stand by the gable of the mill and watch the two large wheels turn. They are called overshot wheels because the water from the mill pond passes through a sluice hitting the top of the wheels. The weight of the water in the wheel buckets rotates the wheels. There is something fascinating about this noisy, splendid demonstration of a simple mechanical principle. However, it is not our intention to transfix visitors by a romantic glimpse of the wheels in their cool shadowy pit. Once inside the mill, it is possible to study more closely how water power is exploited to drive the various machines used for processing grain.

Previous page: The watermill from Funen is idyllically situated at the bottom of a valley. It is low-lying and near water to power its wheels. The wing to the right is the scullery. The mill can be seen behind the roof.

Water to the overshot wheels can be regulated through a hatch in the gable with the help of a long pole to each sluice. Occasionally the miller had to go outside to check the wheels or adjust the sluice at the flood-gate. In this case he went out of the door in the corner just by the mill-race above the wheels. Immediately inside the door is a rye mill, which has also been used for wheat as the cultivation of the latter became a little more widespread. It is the overshot wheel nearest the mill pond that drives this mill. The transmission of power from the shaft of the waterwheel to the mill shaft takes place out of sight under the floor by means of the big pit wheel, which rotates down there in the dark. This wheel drives the vertical shaft which works the upper millstone. But the turning of this millstone is difficult to follow because it is entirely enclosed in a wooden container. Therefore, all that can be seen is the container and a large wooden hopper. Grain was fed into the latter either from a sack or through a chute from the grain loft.

The high millstone in the opposite corner of the mill is a kibbling mill driven by the overshot wheel furthest from the mill pond. There is also a shell mill concealed under the floor. Both of them were used for producing barley groats.

These, then, are the most important components of the assorted machinery of the mill, although much else is to be found. For example, there is a grading machine and a grain cleaner near the stairs, and below the floor an oat crusher. Two types of conveyors are also used, one is a rope sack hoist to take sacks up to the loft, and the other a rotating conveyor which carries the ground meal from the mill to the flour sieve. This flour sieve or boulter is also concealed in a big wooden box; in the boulter is a rotating roller covered with a very fine cloth.

Descriptions of complicated machinery do not usually give an entirely clear picture of working processes. It is better to spend a little time in the mill when it is working, and watch how the cog wheels and pinions interlock to set every component part of a highly complex processing plant into action. A mill must be experienced when it is crowded with the noises of its machinery – the creaking timbers and a low, steady rumble. Even the building vibrates slightly but not too much, for this would indicate that the mill is not functioning correctly.

To the accompaniment of the strange music of the mill the visitor glances around. Here are the utensils of the trade: bushels, sacks, baskets and bins, but there are also items which, when they are explained,

Left: A wooden trough leads the mill race to the wheels. The weight of water in the wheel buckets rotates the wheels.

Opposite page: View of the mill itself. Water flows down from the left from the mill pond and is regulated by two sluices with the help of two long poles to a hatch in the gable.

The scullery in the transverse wing has an open chimney from which the bread oven and copper are stoked. To the left is the corner of a dough trough. The hooks in the beam were used when animals were slaughtered. The door to the right leads to the dairy.

Opposite page: In the foreground is a rye mill. Grain is poured down the chute. The top of the upper millstone can be seen in its wooden container, when it rotates a little of the grain trickles through the hole in the middle through to the millstones, where it is ground and pours out below.

illustrate important aspects of the work of a miller. By the gateway to the courtyard hangs a heavy brake-shoe for horse-drawn wagons, used when heavily laden wagons were driven down the sunken road with their load of grain in sacks. The downward slope of the road was too steep for the horses to hold the wagon, but when the brake-shoe was attached to the wheel, it ground slowly over the gravel much as the runner of a sledge in the same conditions. There is also the toll cup – a round copper scoop with turned wooden handle – which the miller used for measuring out his share of the grain brought in by farmers to be ground. And in the mill room is the miller's desk with his register of customers, the initials of whom recur on all the sacks in the mill loft.

Some of his customers, in any event,

were invited into the mill room while waiting for their grain to be ground. The room was also used by the family normally, notice the play corner in it for the children. Behind the mill room is the kitchen, and if one compares this with most of the other kitchens in the museum, a difference is at once noticeable: the iron range, representing modern comfort in contrast to the raised hearth of the open

152

The front parlour in the miller's home is furnished in the style favoured by well-to-do townspeople at the close of the 19th century.

Opposite page: The kitchen of the Funen watermill seems modern compared with the other kitchens to be seen at the museum. An iron range has been built into the old open chimney.

chimney. The kitchen range is but one of the details in the miller's home to indicate that the era it represents is a slightly later one than that of most of the other buildings in Frilandsmuseet. The separate bedroom with its single beds is another detail, and the upholstered furniture in the "best room", now partially transformed from a room for storing linen etc. to a "front parlour", as well as the small rooms in the attic. The period it represents is the 1890's when the last miller lived there with his family.

However, it is not only the somewhat later period which conveys a different atmosphere to the other homesteads in the museum. That the social position of the miller was a relatively high one in the rural community has also played a role. At any rate millers presumably often felt slightly superior to ordinary farmers who were given a dram in the mill room, although both they and other good people probably never passed beyond this or the scullery and kitchen. Only specially honoured visitors went into the other rooms, or entered the house by the best entrance. Not everybody had the opportunity of sitting in the embroidered occasional chairs with white antimacassars (to protect them against hair oil). The visitor could turn the leaves of the family album and, if really fortunate, listen to the miller's daughter play the harmonium.

154

When the miller and his family gave a party the "best room" at the end of the house was also used. It is a room worth looking at more closely, for here again the difference between the home of the miller and the ordinary farmer is evident. True, the storage furniture is still to be found, but as opposed to the other "best rooms" to be seen at the museum, it is obviously intended to be a comfortable room to sit in. There is a sofa and table, upholstered chairs, a wicker chair and a rocking chair, as well as bric-à-brac, pot plants and curtains at the windows. In other words, it is furnished according to the latest fashion at the close of the 19th century; a parlour in virtually the same style as that in an urban middle-class home of the same period.

Another difference between the water-mill and other farmsteads are the attic rooms in the loft. The greater part of the loft has been used for storing old chests with household linen etc. The girls of the house mangled and pressed washing in the large mangle up here, while the children played exciting games in the gloom. In one gable leading from the loft is the daughter's room, and in the other a spare room for guests.

Shoemaker's Cottage

Not until this yellow half-timbered cottage was put up did the collection of buildings from East Jutland at Frilandsmuseet begin to take on a village-like appearance. For it was then possible to get some idea of a village street because of the way in which the cottage was situated, opposite the large redwashed farmstead, with the whitewashed potter's workshop a little further down the road. It was acquired in Ødis Bramdrup in 1962 and its re-erection at the museum was completed in 1966.

The cottage tells us a little about how the customs of East Jutland and North Schleswig meet and mingle. Ødis Bramdrup lies in one of the so-called "eight parishes" south of Kolding. It is an area which formerly belonged to the Duchy of Schleswig, but after the border war with Germany in 1864 and subsequent frontier realignment, it still remained under Danish sovereignty unlike most of North Schleswig which came under German rule. It is a transitional region not only from a political and administrative point of view. But culturally, too, it is a zone with a mixture of characteristics of both East Jutland and North Schleswig, for example its building traditions and interior arrangement of the home.

The heavy half-timbering and plentiful filling timber are entirely normal features of East Jutland buildings of considerable age. A particular characteristic of the southerly part of Jutland, though, is the bole construction previously used in the building. Admittedly, none of the bays are built in this technique now with horizontal boards between upright posts, but when the building was dismantled for removal to Frilandsmuseet, it was found that a considerable number of the upright posts had grooves in their sides to receive horizontal boards.

Moreover, an examination of the building in connection with its removal revealed that not all of it was equally old. The date 1733, carved in a piece of timber above the door to the stable, is of no dating significance as far as the cottage is concerned. The door in question belongs

Opposite page: The shoemaker's cottage from Ødis Bramdrup looks very idyllic, freshly whitewashed and screened by lilacs. But on closer inspection it is obvious that the occupants were kept busy with repairs.

to a bay which has been added to the stalls, and the timber with the date has in all likelihood come from another building. The other end of the cottage has also been added to. Thus the middle part of the building is the oldest, and probably once a little cottage on its own.

Although small, the original cottage must have been quite an impressive building. The thick uprights and oak planks of the outside walls. The beams were not mortised into the uprights but rested on top of the walls. Elsewhere in Denmark, this feature would indicate a fairly late construction, but in this case it is the normal custom of North Schleswig. The end walls of the cottage terminated in steep wooden gables over a projection supported by corbels.

Of the wealth of traces in this cottage, no single phase could be dated with any certainty. On the other hand, we are able to conclude that the little original cottage does not appear always to have stood on the site in Ødis Bramdrup, where it was found in a very altered state by the museum. There is, namely, some indication that the earliest cottage was moved to the site. It is not known when this occurred, but it appears to have been before 1789. Because in that year, the cottage in its original shortened form appears in a map of the village and its land. The extensions were presumably added after this date.

Therefore there is little to be learned about the history of the building from written records. These, though, are of considerable help in another respect, because they tell us about the people who lived in the cottage. We now know a considerable amount about the occupants from the close of the 1700's until the museum took over the cottage. A common characteristic of the occupants through the years is that they gained their livelihood from two different sources. They farmed on a very modest scale, mostly concentrated on providing fodder for a single cow. And, in addition, they each had a craft or trade of some kind.

The records reveal such occupations as a tailor, a shoemaker – who was followed by an occupant who was both a shoemaker and a clogmaker, and finally a thatcher who was also a home butcher. All were very typical occupations for smallholders who, with too little land to support a family, presumably preferred to specialise in crafts and trades rather than to work as farm labourers.

In any event, the cottage appears to have been the home of a shoemaker from the 1790's to the end of the 1850's. As this is a fairly considerable length of time, the museum was very naturally interested in re-creating the home of a smallholder whose trade was shoemaking. But the difficulty was that a hundred years had elapsed from the time the last shoemaker had retired until the museum took over the cottage. However this problem was solved by moving a shoemaker's workshop from the neighbouring village of Agtrup, likewise in one of the "eight parishes".

Behind the kitchen we can now see the little workshop. The shoemaker has sat in his leather apron on a stool in front of the work table beneath the only window in the room. Here a shaft of light falls on his tools, and the boots and shoes being made. When it grew dark the workshop lamp was lit – a petroleum lamp hanging from the ceiling and fitted with a large tin shade. The shoemaker had all his tools within easy reach in front of him. Shoes to be set aside were put on a shelf with the lasts. Close to the stove on the other side stands a Singer sewing machine, presumably manufactured in 1914.

Both the petroleum lamp and the sewing machine immediately indicate that the workshop is not a very old one. The time had passed when everything was

The shoemaker's work table is directly beneath the window, here was the best light in the day-time. At night he worked by the light of a paraffin lamp. The well-equipped workshop also has a sewing-machine. To the right is a shelf with finished shoes and lasts. Behind the work table is a large roll of leather, and in the niche in the wall are boxes with tacks.

sewn by hand by the light of a crusie lamp – a lamp of this kind was fitted with a glass bulb filled with water, a globe which refracted the rays of light. The present workshop was equipped at a time when technical advances had been made. For example, some of the tools are types presumably introduced into Denmark during the latter half of the 19th century. In short, it was not possible for the museum to find a shoemaker's workshop old enough to correspond with the period when shoemaking was done in the cottage from Ødis Bramdrup. And this of course is hardly surprising.

It can perhaps be said that the chronology of this cottage is a little difficult to define. For there is absolutely no guarantee of contemporaneity covering what is to be seen. Nevertheless, the interior of the cottage has been re-created on the basis of fairly sound evidence. The open chimney in the kitchen, for example, was in an excellent state of preservation, despite the fact that the last occupants had at some time started to use a kitchen range. The alcove beds in the dwelling-room had been transformed into a little lobby, but the front of the alcoves served as the partition wall, and were found in good condition beneath the wallpaper. Indeed, everything has been arranged either according to traces found in the building, or information supplied by the oldest surviving members of the family who had lived in the cottage. One of the

informants related how he had slept in the cottage as a child when his grandparents lived there, because his own home nearby was overcrowded with children. He could remember, for example, the arrangement of the table and chairs in the dwelling-room. This was characteristic of the area, because both here and in North Schleswig generally the custom of fixed benches was abandoned at a fairly early date in favour of chairs grouped round the table. He could also remember the furnishing of the "best room" before it was turned into a bedroom. He described the garden, and mentioned a bench where the family sat by the sun-warmed gable wall with its view across the vegetable patch and currant bushes to the little stream, where water was collected before a pump and well were installed.

The cottage from Ødis Bramdrup now stands in fairly good condition, surrounded very much as formerly by trees and bushes and with a farmstead as its neighbour. That it seems somewhat more idyllic at Frilandsmuseet, though, than was actually the case cannot be avoided. This impression is modified when we hear about the water supply, sanitation, and how the occupants dealt with the problems of rotting half-timbering and dilapidation. In fact, how daily difficulties both large and small were overcome.

It is on just these points that museum techniques fail to give a realistic impression of conditions as they really were in a little cottage like this in bygone days. If a building is to be preserved it cannot be allowed to fall into disrepair, and as for the way of life of countryfolk who lived in these conditions, we must appeal to the imagination of those who visit Frilandsmuseet. That with the help of clues provided by the museum in the form of furnishings and interior arrangement, they can visualise what the home would be like if it were still inhabited.

The Bole Barn

The term used to describe this building may sound curious to most ears, but it in fact means a barn built in the bole technique with horizontal planks or thick boards laid on top of each other between upright posts. It was a widespread building method in the past. In recent times most buildings of this type were to be found in the former Danish provinces of Sweden and in an area in the southerly

Previous page: The gable of the bole barn from Grønning-hoved is steep and impressive. It terminates at the top in a so-called "fire rod", a decorative vertical rod sometimes believed to prevent fire.

Right: Rafters going up for the bole barn from Sparlund. Some are already in position, the rest are stacked ready for use in the foreground.

part of the east coast of Jutland. That other areas have also had buildings like this is demonstrated by the farmsteads from Sønder Sejerslev and Læsø, which both contain some walling of this type. The South Swedish bole construction is represented by the farmsteads from Halland and northerly Scania. The type from South-Eastern Jutland, on the other hand, has so far been represented solely by a barn from Grønninghoved, a village close to Skamlingsbanken in the parish of Vejstrup, one of the "eight parishes" south of Kolding.

This barn has had a somewhat chequered career at Frilandsmuseet. It came to the museum in 1918, and here it was incorporated in a composite farmstead, the farmstead from North Schleswig, one of the drawbacks of which being that the dwelling-house was not originally that of a farmstead. The result was not very satisfactory, but at the time the chances of acquiring a complete farmstead from the region could not be exploited. Later, the barn stood alone in the south-easterly corner of the museum, where it was used for storing building timber. Neither was this solution satisfactory, but it was part of a plan for developing this part of the muse-

um park. However, this plan, like the original position of the barn, had to be relinquished when revised plans were drawn up to deal with the additional land taken over by the museum.

The latest idea is to give visitors an impression of the bole houses of South-East Jutland by building a new composite farmstead. This is obviously something of an emergency measure, but it is no longer possible to find a complete farmstead of this kind. Yet there are so many important characteristics in the building traditions of this area of North Schleswig, particularly bole houses, that the region must undoubtedly be represented. The farmstead will be pieced together from buildings already in store at the museum, and this time the dwelling-house will be that of a farmstead. It comes from the island of Barsø and was acquired by the museum in 1954; its re-erection commenced in 1972. A wing of the farmstead from Grønninghoved will also be incorporated, as well as a barn from Sparlund. This bole barn comes from Øsby parish south of Haderslev Fjord. It was acquired in 1930, but not re-erected at the museum until 1972.

The Ostenfeld Farmstead

When one approaches this farmstead, one can immediately see that it differs from all the other farmsteads in the museum. Its size and dimensions are utterly different to the long, low buildings close by. The large gateway in one end of the building is also unusual.

Over the gateway is an inscription with a date and the owner's name. The date 1685 is by Danish standards of great age for a rural building. Parts of the building, judging from other dates here and there in the house, are however later. The name Hans Petersen seems to have a sound Danish ring about it, but hasty conclusions should not be drawn about the prevalence of Danish names in the area because of this, although the place the farmstead comes from may tempt one to do so.

Ostenfeld is situated in South Schleswig between the towns of Husum and Schleswig, slightly west of the centre of the region. The village lies on geest land – dry land as opposed to the marshes. It is in one of the parishes just north of the marsh and meadowland bordering the river Trene, which continues the line of the ancient Danevirke ramparts westwards. It is therefore natural to ask whether reasons of nationalism influenced the choice at the time of this particular farmstead. For when it was acquired in 1899 and opened in 1901 as one of the first buildings to be erected on the newly acquired museum land in Lyngby, the 1864 war was still an open wound and Danish nationalism a heartfelt cause.

Bernhard Olsen and others obviously had quite special feelings in connection with the removal of this farmstead to

Previous page: The gateway in the gable and proportions of the Ostenfeld farmstead are strange and striking even at distance.

the museum of buildings in Lyngby, where it would serve as a magnificent monument to the territory lost. On the other hand, the choice is surprising as it was particularly unsuited to illustrate how deep Danish roots were in this region. A true illustration would have been the choice of an undeniably Danish building type from a locality as far south as possible. Instead one of the most northerly examples was chosen of a distinctly German type of building. It would seem to indicate that there were quite other reasons for the selection of this farmstead. The thoughts that lay behind the removal of the farmstead from Ostenfeld were primarily governed by the desire to show the evolution of the peasant dwelling from a simple habitation to a more complex one.

The two decisive factors for the selection of the farmstead was the absence of a chimney and the propinquity of man and beast in a building common to both. These are indeed the most striking features upon entering the building. The strangeness conveyed by its exterior is at once confirmed within. And the same traits have continued to fascinate those who visit it ever since the farmstead has been at the museum. This curious building steeped with the echoes of a bygone way of life, so different from that of today, has a very special power of attraction. How many people are there who, after a fleeting visit to Frilandsmuseet some years back, only remember that they saw a large hall once shared by man and beast? Tourists returning home from a quick visit to the museum during which they have seen the Ostenfeld farmstead, and possibly one or two more of the most striking buildings, for example the farmsteads from Eiderstedt and Halland, must receive a curious impression of how Danish peasants lived in the old days.

Even though the Ostenfeld farmstead may seem confusing, for the more thought-

ful museum visitor it has in fact an important mission, as together with the Eiderstedt farmstead, which arrived later, it shows what farmsteads in a neighbouring region looked like. By very reason of the difference it accentuates the common features of all the other buildings in the museum, for these against such a background are all of the Danish or Scandinavian types, while the Ostenfeld and Eiderstedt farmsteads represent something more Continental.

The Ostenfeld farmstead is of the Saxon or Low Saxon type which is again part of a larger category with the same construction, a nave forming a large hall flanked by two side aisles, widespread throughout North Germany. As mentioned, the characteristic features are the gateway in the gable facing the road, the large broad building with its great diver-

sity of functions under the same roof, and the hearth without a chimney.

The large room with clay floor fills most of the building. Grain was threshed here, but apart from being a threshing floor it also served as a fodder bay where feed for the animals was got ready. It was easy to feed the livestock as their stalls were ranged down each side of the room in the side aisles or outshots – between the uprights supporting the wall plate and the outside wall. Cows were tied facing into the room in the custom for Saxon-type buildings as opposed to the Danish practice. We miss the row of cows looking into the room, and in other respects, too, the large room is emptier than it has been, as hay and straw were stored in the loft above, and over the cow stalls, as well as on part of the clay floor.

In the end of the nave furthest from the entrance is the living accommodation. Here, as well, there is a stall-like recess in the outshots, one on either side, with a table beneath the window and a bench on each side, and an alcove bed behind. At bedtime the people grouped round the table could turn round and crawl into bed! The hearth is in the middle of the floor, a square of cobbles on which the fire burned. Firewood was propped against a wrought iron fire-dog in order to allow a draught to feed the fire from below. A cooking pot hangs over the hearth from an adjustable hook which can be raised and lowered at will. A kettle hook hangs from a horizontal rod resting on beams above the hearth. This type of house often had a chimney-crane in the form of a horizontal arm attached to a post, like the one we see here, beside the hearth. As there is no chimney, smoke from the fire had to find its way out as best it could, a small opening above the entrance has provided an outlet. Nevertheless, in the autumn and winter months when the loft was full of hay, a lot of smoke must have hung thickly under the beams, gradually seeping out through the side doors and gateway. In a nave house like this one, a strong smell of smoke and soot has intermingled with the usual smells of a byre, and it was said that the cows in Ostenfeld would only eat smoked hay.

Later Saxon houses, however, did not remain within the limits of one large room with many collective functions. At the rear of the Ostenfeld farmstead are two additional rooms which not only improve the dwelling quarters but which, through the furniture and fittings in them, convey an impression of what must have been a fairly prosperous environment.

One of the rooms can be heated by an extension stove, and it is this room, first and foremost, which illustrates a break from the traditions of the early Saxon collective room common to man and beast, for here the farmer and his family could withdraw and lead a life of greater refinement, which must have eventually set them apart from those whose place were the seats about the hearth. Farmhands had presumably no occasion to enter the fine tiled room with carved alcove beds.

The other room could not be heated, neither does it represent any change of tradition, for it was primarily used for storing things in, hence the chests and cupboards. But the Ostenfeld farmstead, being as it is, one of the oldest farmsteads in Frilandsmuseet, and coming as it does from a very old-fashioned region, these types of furniture are all exceedingly old. It is a room where parties could be held, and where many people could be seated. The large table chest by the end wall could be laid, and smaller tables too, while the necessary serving dishes and plates were at hand in a row above the panelling.

In-fillings of the gateway gable between the half-timbering are bricked up in patterns. The timbering was once blue.

167

The Eiderstedt Farmstead

The marshland farmstead from Eiderstedt with its high-pitched roof in the flat landscape of the northerly part of the museum can be seen from far away. It comes from a region very different to that in which it now stands in North Zealand. But the farmstead is a good example of how the museum can create a setting for an old building which gives an impression of its native locality.

The first thing one notices is the dyke which surrounds the site. It is a drainage dyke which corresponds to that which enclosed the farmstead on its original site. The area within the dyke is raised above the surrounding terrain beyond. It is an artificial mound, known as a *varf*, on which farmsteads in low-lying marshland were built to protect them from flooding should the water level in this flat area rise.

Round the mound are meadows. In Eiderstedt the fens, as these meadows are called, are enclosed in a network of dykes as far as the eye can see. There are gates or stiles at the intersections but no other form of fencing is necessary. The cattle grazing in the meadows had nothing to rub themselves against, and therefore a scratching post was put up. The museum has also done this a little to the north of the farmstead. Another object which is very much part of this characteristic landscape leans near the door to the threshing floor. It is a long pole – an essential aid when living in the marshes – as only by using this was it possible to jump far enough to cross the dykes.

Previous page: The Eiderstedt farmstead comes from a marshland region. Like many marsh farmsteads it is built on an artificial mound surrounded by drainage dykes and low-lying meadows. At the centre is the entrance to the threshing floor and barn, to the left the door to the cowshed and stables, and to the right the door to the living quarters.

Those who wish to visit the farmstead, however, do not have to indulge in any athletics as there is a crossing through a gate so that the visitor can reach the *varf* in comfort. Other gates and stiles can also be used as there is a foothold on one side of the gatepost.

The first impression of the farmstead is striking at a distance, overwhelming near at hand. Alone by its shape, size and pitch of its massive roof, it is different to all other buildings in the museum, and manifestly a building type which is totally dissimilar to what is otherwise seen here. Like the Ostenfeld farmstead, it represents a type of building native to a neighbouring region and not Danish. But by their very strangeness both farmsteads help to illustrate the likeness shared by the rest of the farmsteads and cottages in the museum. The Nordic dwelling borders on two very distinct house types in South Schleswig. The farmstead from Ostenfeld – one of the museum's earliest acquisitions – is a nave house. The farmstead from Kating on the Eiderstedt peninsula, jutting into the North Sea in the extreme southwesterly corner of South Schleswig, was not acquired until 1956 and not opened until 1960. It is an example of the house type known as *haubarg*.

Characteristic for the *haubarg* are its lofty dimensions, both functionally and structurally. Everything is gathered beneath a single roof which is large and high. As the ridge is quite short, the shape of the roof is almost pyramidal. One side of the almost square building can have a slightly lower roof, though, which protrudes over the end of the living quarters. Thus one side of the square contains the dwelling-rooms, and the rest of the interior is outhouse accommodation. An impressive timber construction carries the roof of this large building.

This structure is best seen from the barn in the middle of the building, for

Previous page: The Eiderstedt farmstead is a type of building known as a hauparg. The entire farmstead is beneath one large roof carried by an interesting timber structure of four tall posts supporting a heavy horizontal timber frame. The construction is shown in the sketch to the right. The colour plate to the left is a view from the threshing floor just inside the double doors to the square between the four tall roof posts, one of which is in the immediate foreground to the left. The square is barn space where crops could be stored, right up to the roof if necessary, which is why it is separated from the loft over the living quarters by wooden bars.

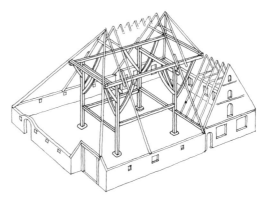

at each corner of the barn is an exceptionally tall and heavy post, indeed the barn is called "the square". The posts carry a heavy horizontal timber frame which is rectangular in shape, and from which the main rafters run up to the ridge. The frame projects a greater distance over the two posts on one side, in order to carry the roof over the broader living quarters.

The *hauparg* is a usual type of farmstead in the Eiderstedt peninsula, but it is also found elsewhere. North of Eiderstedt in the marshes of West Schleswig a few sporadic examples are known, and it occurs together with related farmstead types in considerable numbers further to the south and south-west. It is usually considered to be a construction which originated in the Netherlands, and the result of a gradual course of development over a period. The theory being that it evolved at the close of the 16th and beginning of the 17th centuries during a period of general prosperity in Europe, with rising corn prices which Dutch farmers in the marshlands knew how to exploit – the increasing corn exports presumably necessitated larger barns. The *hauparg* is believed to owe its shape to the joining of a dwelling-house with what was originally a detached barn.

There is every indication that this theory is correct, moreover it agrees very well with what is otherwise known of the cultural influences along these low-lying coastal marshlands. In any event, the *hauparg* reached the fertile Eiderstedt peninsula where crops were heavy and large barns needed. The museum's *hauparg* appears to have existed in its present form since 1653, according to the date in iron-ties on the south gable of the living quarters. However, parts of the building are older. The iron-ties spell out initials as well as giving the date, and this supports the theory of a Dutch influence. A A H stands for Adriaen Alberts Hauwert who was mayor of the town called Medemblik in the province of North Holland. This far distant absentee landowner owned the farmstead in the mid-1600's, and it was not till the close of the century that it passed out of the hands of his family.

The gable with the date and initials is also extremely Dutch in appearance. It is divided by horizontal moulded courses in the brickwork, and with three arched apertures down the middle, the lowest of which has a hatch into the loft. The entrance is to one side in this gable, but it is not the only way of entering the building. The most striking entrance gives on to the threshing floor, but the double doors were normally closed to keep out the westerly winds. There is also a stable door, and a door out of the back by the scullery. But the best entrance is the one in the south gable leading into the passage hall.

171

This broad passage has a variety of functions. Apart from being a hall, it contains chests and wardrobes for storing clothes, a table and bench where meals could be eaten, and in the wall behind the bench are cupboard beds with shutters where farmhands slept. The rear of the passage is separated from the front by a partition wall with a door leading into it. It has been used as a scullery, but there is also an alcove bed where maidservants slept. Sundry butter and cheese-making equipment can be seen, such as butter and cheese moulds. The scullery is practically situated for this work, with the byre on one side and the kitchen on the other.

The open chimney with raised hearth in the kitchen is not unusual, but it should be noticed that beneath the hearth is a bread oven. This is a characteristic of hearths in the coastal lowlands to the west in North and South Schleswig. The inaccessible position of the oven at floor level made it necessary to stand in a hole in the floor in front of it when baking. The hole was covered with a wooden lid when not in use. Leading from the kitchen is a raised larder above a cellar. A detail in the cellar illustrates how far we are here from native Danish environments, for the niches in the cellar have been used for storing wine in.

Indeed, there is undeniably an impression that the Eiderstedt farmer had links with the outside world, and that the daily life of the farmstead contained slightly more refinements than those of most Danish farmsteads. The heated dwelling-room beside the kitchen heightens this impression. It is the family's own room, and it is highly unlikely that the farmhands in the hall outside went to and fro from their table into this room.

The furnishing of the dwelling-room is a good example of the many features of interior arrangement which predominated along the North Sea coast in the past, regardless of national frontiers. The walls are covered with Frisian and Dutch tiles, those by the door are decorated with birds, while those by the stove (heated from the kitchen) make up a colourful vase with flowers. The hanging clock is a Frisian type often encountered along the coast, its sides are decorated with mermaids. The room, however, should not be judged solely as a place to display applied art, because it was above all where the family gathered when they were not working elsewhere in the building. The farmer and his wife slept in the alcove bed with carved doors. Meals were eaten now and then at the table, if the family did not join the servants at the long table in the hall. And if the farmer came home late from a business trip, food was kept warm for him on the stove under a curfew (from the French *couvre feu*) – a rounded metal cover, originally used to extinguish embers. If he were chilled and tired after travelling through the windy marshland, he could rest in the armchair near the warmth of the stove. One or two guests could be served a hot toddy here from the toddy cups in the hanging cupboard above the desk.

On the other hand, if there were many guests to be entertained the "best room" next door was used, and although it had no stove it could be heated with a brazier, a portable flat iron container for embers, or a foot-warmer could be collected, a little pierced box of brass used in the same way, and comfortable to have by the feet. Women put it under their skirts if they had to sit for a long time in an unheated room. Otherwise the "best room" served as a place for storing clothing and linen in cupboards and chests.

Opposite page: The living-room in the Eiderstedt farmstead immediately gives an impression of prosperity. It in many ways illustrates the high standard of homes along the North Sea coast.

172

Farmstead From Sønder Sejerslev

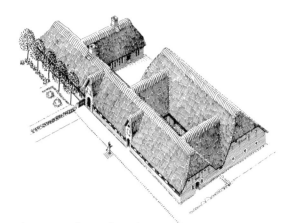

That this is a large farmstead can be seen from some distance away, particularly if one approaches it from the south. From this angle the full length of the long wing containing the dwelling-house and cow-shed can be appreciated, with the roof of the barn behind rising above it. The barn is parallel to the cowshed and connected with it by two short cross-wings, thus forming a small courtyard. There is one more cross-wing behind at the dwelling-house end. All in all a farmstead of complicated structure with many component parts. Calculated on the area of the roofing, it is one of the largest buildings in the museum. This is a very apt basis for calculations when it is known that the task of thatching it entailed tying the thatch to about two miles of laths in the roof.

One of the largest farmsteads at Frilandsmuseet, but the one with the smallest courtyard! However, both the complicated complex of buildings and the courtyard without a function are characteristic for the extreme south-westerly region of North Schleswig, where the farmstead was acquired in 1962. It was opened at the museum in 1971.

The region from which it comes has a building tradition that differs in many ways from the rest of the country. This is due to local conditions, particularly geographical and occupational. Moreover, the close cultural links with the other regions along the North Sea coast, where conditions were fairly similar, have also played a role. Communications along the coast were good and provided a natural passage for cultural renewal. The resemblance between buildings in the westerly regions north and south of the present Danish/German frontier is some-times explained as being the result of a Frisian influence. Yet some of the structural features are found in more widespread regions than those which came directly under the Frisian influence. This applies to the dark red brick walls and dormers above the doors, as well as the long main wing containing the dwelling and cowshed. The barn parallel to it occurs frequently, often extending beyond the end of the main wing, as was originally the case in the present farmstead. A later extension to the cowshed here included the cross-wings to the barn, with the little courtyard as a result.

The most striking difference between the cottages and farmsteads of southwesterly Denmark and those in the rest of the country is the early date at which bricks were used for outside walls. Brickmaking in Denmark dates back to the middle of the 12th century when, during the reign of Valdemar the Great, Valdemar's Wall at Danevirke, St. Bendt's Church in Ringsted on Zealand, and some other Romanesque buildings were built of bricks. However, this building material was not used in rural buildings during the centuries that followed, and not until the mid-19th century did bricks come into general use for building in the countryside. There are two factors which explain why bricks were adopted in southwesterly Denmark as early as the 1600's

The farmstead from Sønder Sejerslev, seen here in mid-winter, is a fairly large complex of buildings as shown in the drawing on the previous page. The colour plate is of the long wing containing the dwelling, stables and cowshed. Behind the latter to the right the barn can be seen.

to become widespread in the 1700's, firstly a chronic shortage of timber in the area and secondly, a cultural influence from the south-west where burnt clay had long been used as a building material in the Netherlands.

In some of the oldest brick buildings preserved in West Schleswig until fairly recently, traces of an earlier structure have been found, e.g. old upright posts encased in brickwork. This also applies to the farmstead from Sønder Sejerslev at Frilandsmuseet, for in the walls of the cowshed some uprights were found with grooves in their sides for horizontal boards. Today, the walls of the barn give some idea of the construction, as the relics found

in situ there enabled us to reconstruct this building method in order to illustrate that, in spite of its prodigious consumption of timber, it has existed even here in the extreme west in bygone times.

Indeed, as we have seen, the appearance of the farmstead has changed in the course of the centuries. But this is perfectly usual as in many ways rural buildings may be likened to living organisms, growing a little here or a little there, while another part of the building may be falling into disrepair, eventually to disappear entirely. The farmstead from Sønder Sejerslev has not only sloughed its skin, so to speak, as wooden walls were replaced by bricks. By degrees it has also become larger. Dates on cottages and farmsteads are therefore to be treated with a certain reservation. The dates 1779 and 1823 on the iron-ties of the gables of the Sønder

Harness and fodder boxes etc. are kept in the passage between the stables and an extra byre. A glimpse into the farmhands' room reveals more harness and the chests in which they kept their belongings.

Opposite page: The smallest farmyard at Frilandsmuseet is to be found in the Sønder Sejerslev farmstead. It had no purpose but was the result of an extension to the cowshed end.

Sejerslev farmstead give the dates of extensions and rebuilding, possibly simply the bricking-up of the gables. The greater part of the buildings is undoubtedly older.

The reason for enlarging the farmstead was of course to gain more space, and there is no doubt what it was needed for. The barn is fairly large and one of the oldest buildings on the farm, therefore storage space has not been a pressing problem. But when the buildings were examined in connection with their removal to the museum, it was clear that the cowshed had been extended several times.

The disposition of a farmstead's buildings is closely related to the farming patterns of the locality. Here, like many other farmsteads in the region, cattle-rearing was the primary occupation. This explains the size of the cowshed, which has not only been lengthened several

times but supplemented by an additional cowshed in one end of the barn. When spring came it was essential to have as many bullocks as possible to let out into the fens in the marshes belonging to the farm. The bullocks were sold later at market in either Tønder, Husum or Hamburg.

We have been fortunate enough to learn about the economy of the farm from two account books. One is just a small notebook with notes of cattle sales for a number of years during the 19th century until the 1870's. This gives some

idea of what must have been a considerable source of income for this fairly prosperous farmer who, during this period, owned and ran two farms. The other account book dates back to the first half of the 18th century. It gives a picture primarily of the economy of the farmstead excluding farming.

It reveals that the farmer had financial interests in pursuits other than farming. At one time he had an interest in shipping along the North Sea coast, and in connection with this, took part in what was an early form of marine insurance. All this led to prosperity on the farm. The old account book shows how money bred money. In any event, a not insignificant measure of prosperity resulted from the farmer's activities as money-lender to the local population. It was before savings banks were introduced in Denmark at

On a farm such as that from Sønder Sejerslev where bullock rearing was the major source of income, the stalls for young cattle in the cowshed were the most important part of the outbuildings. Bullocks were fattened in the fen meadows but breeding stock wintered in the cowshed with the rest of the herd.

the beginning of the 19th century. Those who had money to spare either had to hide it in the bottom of a chest, or earn interest by lending it to others. Neither practice was entirely without risk.

His earnings from farming, however, were not solely supplemented by so-called unearned incomes through investment. For a number of years during the first half of the 18th century a trade was also carried on in the farmstead, namely clockmaking, and the farmer at that time appears to have been a fairly proficient clockmaker. Several entries in the ledger cover clockmaking, and unlike the other activities mentioned in the entries, clock-

178

The table is laid for coffee in the parlour which was arranged after the rebuilding in 1874. The dwelling-room next door and the parlour, are heated by the same large stove with an iron base and tiled top.

making has left tangible evidence which can be seen in the dwelling-house of the farmstead to this day. The finest clock known to be made by the farmer is not here, though, but in the manor-house of Schackenborg for which it was presumably commissioned, for the farm was a copyholding under this estate between 1672 and 1847. A slightly smaller but nevertheless superior grandfather clock can be seen in the dwelling-room where it stood until a few years before the museum acquired the farmstead, and to which it has fortunately been returned. A copy of the third known example but smaller piece of work is also displayed in one of the rooms. It is a brass sun

dial dated 1724 and signed like the other two. When the sun shines into the room visitors can walk over to the window sill on which it stands to see what the time is.

Time-keeping was something which became more widespread during the first half of the 18th century. Sundials and clocks were not solely items acquired by the well-to-do for reasons of prestige – status symbols. A need can be felt to know the exact time in busy surroundings with many activities to control such as this farmstead. The environment of a local upper class – prosperous folk with cattle in the pastures and ships at sea.

But time passes and conditions change. The descendants of those who once lived on the farm will be surprised to hear the word "prosperity" used in this context. For the impression they have of their grandparents and great-grandparents is

On the window sill in one of the rooms is a brass sun dial bearing the date 1724. The sun dial and the grandfather clock in the room beside it were both made by the farmer who at that time was also a clockmaker.

one of thrift and restraint, at any rate compared with modern life. It is a period some faintly recollect hearing about, a time when great changes occurred, when a peasant remained simply a peasant although he traded cattle, and the threshold had been reached between the old subsistence economy and the new money economy.

The museum has chosen to represent a period in the 1870's as the basis for the arrangement and furnishings of the interior, as it corresponds to the phase in the development of the farmstead which can be most accurately portrayed. It is important to know, for example, that the dwelling-house was altered in 1874, the date given in a so-called parish chronicle which recorded items of news, both large and small, in the parish for a number of years in the 19th century. The kitchen must have been modernised at the same time, cooking is now done on an iron range beside a closed chimney. The scullery still has an open chimney, but the bread oven has disappeared, as this was no longer necessary when there were several bakers in the village, where all kinds of bread could be bought.

The modernisation in 1874 also included refurnishing the dwelling-room in the latest fashion. These pieces of furniture stand once more in their original positions. They are veneered and upholstered, and not particularly countrified. The table is laid for a coffee party with the home-made specialities of North Schleswig – a tradition which really took root in the post-war period after 1864, when the Danish population was fighting to preserve its national identity.

The larder has a sunken floor. Food and brewing utensils are kept here.

The little cottage from Nørre Sejerslev was a lace school. It is very similar to many small houses in the Tønder area in appearance, and also in the way the interior is fully utilised. The entrance at the middle leads to the main dwelling. To the right is the entrance to the cowshed. A door in the gable by the cowshed leads to rooms where the retired occupant lived.

Lace School From
Nørre Sejerslev

It is quite possible that some people were rather astonished when Frilandsmuseet acquired a cottage in the village of Nørre Sejerslev in 1965, as it was the neighbouring village in the south-westerly corner of North Schleswig to Sønder Sejerslev, where the large farmstead already described had been acquired. Surely one farmstead was sufficient to represent this region? It even came from the same parish as the lace school.

There were, however, good reasons for the action, because when the cottage from Nørre Sejerslev was re-erected and opened in 1972, two closely related buildings could be seen opposite each other in the museum. They are both expressions of the same local building tradition, and they both represent very much the same period. Their differences, then, are due neither to region nor period, but must be sought for in existing social conditions. By showing two buildings from the same period and area it is possible to demonstrate very clearly the influence of social conditions on the arrangement of a dwelling and working premises. The occupants of the farmstead and cottage respectively have each played an entirely different role in the economical system of the region.

The mutual building traditions of the farmstead from Sønder Sejerslev and the cottage from Nørre Sejerslev can be seen even at a glance. First and foremost the outer walls of brick, as before 1800 it was very unusual for ordinary countryfolk to build in brick. This rule applies to every region of Denmark with the exception of the south-westerly corner of the country. This exception applies to both farmer and smallholder.

If one stands midway between these two buildings from the same parish, a glance from one to the other confirms that the bricks in both are exactly the same dark shade of red. Other mutual features also spring to the eye. For example, both have a hipped roof, i.e. a roof that in addition to sloping down to the two side walls also slopes to the gable wall. The dormer above the entrance is also a characteristic detail. The local dialect word *arkengaf* to describe this opening into the loft of a building is a composite word: arch + gap. Crops were pushed into the loft through this opening. A dormer above the entrance also safeguarded the entrance if there were a fire, in that it prevented burning roofing from sliding down and blocking the door.

The exterior of the house from Nørre Sejerslev, then, clearly demonstrates that we are in the same district as that from which the large farmstead opposite comes. Yet it is not perhaps quite so evident that they belong to the same period. Both buildings are considerably older than their interior arrangement suggests. This is not unusual. For houses built during the 1700's often underwent several interior alterations at later periods. It is frequently an interior dating from the 1800's which provides Frilandsmuseet with the best basis for re-creating the inside of a home. It is also true in the case of the Nørre Sejerslev cottage, and it is fortunate that the two buildings from the same region merge

so naturally in period. Often, though, it is a matter of choosing between several possibilities when deciding which phase in the history of a building is to be represented. In this particular case a direct comparison between the two buildings is considered justified because both have interiors which date back to the period c. 1875.

The most striking difference is in size. The farmstead is a large, extensive complex of buildings, while the cottage is humble, though compact and concentrated and every nook and cranny within the building is fully utilised.

This is evident, for example, in the rooms of the retired smallholder behind the little cowshed. There is not much room here for the old folk to move about in although this may not have been very necessary. The narrowest spot of all is the entrance in the gable and a source of difficulty, too, when the old occupants travelled on their last journey. Indeed, it was stipulated in the tenancy agreement that in this event the coffins would be allowed through the entrance in the front of the house, in order to avoid tipping the coffin. But this stipulation does not appear to have ceremonial implications as the entrance to the cowshed was probably used.

Another example of space saving is the little cowshed where the smallholder's only cow was kept. And under the low roof in the gable outshot is a pigsty for a single pig. A comparison between this cowshed and that of the Sønder Sejerslev farmstead throws the economic differences between the two homesteads into sharp relief. The smallholder had not land enough to keep more livestock, and its modest yield in grain and fodder could easily be stored in the loft.

Opposite page: The lace-making room in the Nørre Sejerslev cottage should be full of people. The lace-maker has sat in the armchair surrounded by her young pupils on stools.

It was therefore fortunate that there were other means of earning a livelihood. In this part of the country, in the area round Tønder, lace was made, and it was to no mean extent a cottage industry sustained by the women from the smallholding milieu. As in other areas where certain forms of handicraft were specialised in, it provided many humble homes with an extra income. But it would be wrong to assume that those engaged in lace-making were able to rise above their class because of it. Although a lace-maker was sometimes considered a good match there were limits to how much she could earn.

This was partly due to the organisation of lace-making in the Tønder area, for it was a cottage industry under entrepreneurs who collected the finished lace, marketing it either direct or through middlemen. The entrepreneurs or their contacts often took the initiative of commissioning work, and they also supplied the lace-makers with yarn and patterns.

Obviously the position of the women making lace was normally marked by a considerable degree of dependence upon the entrepreneurs. The individual lace-maker had little opportunity of coming into direct contact with her customers, and consequently had virtually no chance of influencing the price paid for her work. When times were good a lace-maker could perhaps afford a cottage of her own, if she were particularly fortunate. But the entrepreneurs, each employing hundreds of women throughout the villages and countryside, sometimes became extremely prosperous. It was due to their efforts, however, that Tønder lace became famous with a market that extended far beyond the Danish frontier.

The museum's cottage from Nørre Se-jerslev has experienced both the good times and the bad for Tønder lace. The 1860's and 1870's, the period to which the interior corresponds most closely, represent the final decades of lace-making. Its decline, though, had set in long before despite the fact that the use of lace, for trimming fashionable clothes in the 18th century, continued but to a lesser extent in the 19th century for trimming the clothes of countrywomen. When in the 1840's the lace trade adopted a policy to establish lace schools with the full agreement of the State, a measure already taken in Saxony and Belgium, it was in an effort to aid a profession in difficulties.

The cottage at Frilandsmuseet is a lace school of this kind. It is a typical smallholder's cottage, but the room behind the kitchen is arranged for teaching lace-making. In here the housewife, and ultimately probably an old retired lace-maker, taught a group of young girls the art of lace-making, in the same way as in many a small home in the region. Each girl had a stool and lace pillow, and in the evenings they worked by the light of candles, using glass bulbs filled with water in order to refract the light from the candles.

The art of lace-making had to be learnt as a child if sufficient dexterity were to be acquired for working the lace bobbins. Fingers were no longer nimble enough once they were used for rougher work. The attitude to child labour in those days was different to ours, but clergymen complained that lace-making affected the children's schooling. It is easy to imagine that the work had a bad effect on the health of the girls, sitting still as they had to for hours at a time, bent over work with minute details in a poor light.

The Rømø farmstead seen from the angle in which the barn gable is nearest. The date on it only relates to that end. The two small half-moon windows ventilate the barn in order to dry the crops stored there. Between them a disused buoy has been made into a nesting box.

Skipper's Farmstead From Rømø

Rømø is the most southerly island in Denmark off the North Sea coast, and this farmstead was donated to Frilandsmuseet in 1936 and opened there in 1940, as the first building to be re-erected on the new land made accessible that year. For the first time it was possible to enjoy the additional space when re-creating the surroundings of the farmstead.

The magnificent scenery of Rømø cannot of course be transplanted to Frilandsmuseet. But a little heather may remind

visitors of the moorland at the centre of the island, between the dunes to the west and the salt marshes to the east. The old settlements on Rømø followed a line north/south behind the east coast. The present farmstead was situated in Toftum, not far from a farmstead now a museum in situ The National Museum's *Kommandørgården,* and from this farmstead the others could be reached along a sandy track running up the length of the island. The paths of Frilandsmuseet can be very

185

dusty at times, but they only give a faint idea of what it was like to journey by road in the old days. The only form of road repair on Rømø, before it was connected with the mainland by a long embankment, was to fill the worst holes with branches of heather. On the other hand, an impression could be given at Frilandsmuseet of how the dunes and drift sand on Rømø in many places spread inland to homesteads, even settling up against the buildings. The little kale patch between the dunes in front of the Rømø farmstead at the museum tells us a little of the difficulties of farming and gardening in such conditions. During periods of serious drift sand encroachment there was little chance of keeping the small fields between the dunes free of sand. Indeed, old fields smothered by sand can still be seen here and there on the island. Farming was a hard and unrewarding occupation. In addition, the seafaring traditions of the islanders, as in many other similar communities, meant that a substantial part of the working population was absent for long periods at a time, and the task of battling the mean recalcitrant forces of nature thus fell primarily to the women.

As we shall see, there is a certain discrepancy between these difficult external conditions and the prosperity displayed by the highly developed interiors of many farmsteads on Rømø. The contrast is perhaps not so striking when a farmstead is seen from the outside. The brick built walls date back in many cases to the time when seafaring provided an extra means of income, it is true. However, the dark red brick walls are not in themselves characteristic of the island but of the entire south-westerly part of Jutland.

Previous page: "Behold ourselves and the heritage bestowed on us by Our Lord" is the inscription on a stone entrance post beneath a relief of the farmer, his wife and son.

Neither is there anything particularly impressive about the outward appearance of the average Rømø farmstead – huddled close to the ground, with a hipped roof protecting it from the constant westerly winds and blending with the landscape.

The Rømø farmstead at the museum has a T-shaped ground-plan, and when seen from the outside the dates in iron-ties on the gables may seem a little confusing. The west wing, containing the cowshed, stable and barn, was apparently built in two stages – the north end in 1773 and the south end in 1793 – but it is actually two cross-wings added to each side of the west gable of the dwelling-house. The east gable of the dwelling-house, on the other hand, bears the date 1862. When one enters the dwelling-house it is clear that something is wrong, for it is in fact the oldest part of the farmstead – the date on the gable simply denotes the year in which a new brick gable was put up.

This is obviously not the only structural alteration to have been carried out during the course of the years. The most radical change was undoubtedly when the half-timbering and wattle and daub walls were replaced by bricks, presumably during a big wave of structural improvements that swept the island and neighbouring districts on the mainland. Some impression of what the farmstead looked like before being rebuilt in brick can be gained from the north side of the dwelling-house. Here, as well as in the east side of the cowshed wing, are preserved some of the uprights of the half-timbering.

At this corner to the north is the entrance to the scullery, situated in the wing containing the cowshed that was added to the early cowshed at the end of the dwelling-house. The main entrance leads into a flag stone passage which divides the living quarters from the stable. It is marked in fine style by two sandstone posts

The winter living-room – facing south – at the Rømø farmstead, with hanging compass to the left and a model ship on the wall. The walls are covered with either tiles or painted panelling. Next door the walls are red.

with inscriptions and figures carved in relief in 1767. The figures on one are those of the farmer, his wife and son. The posts have the same shape as the porch stones which marked the entrance of old town houses in the past, they are also related to gravestones bearing reliefs of ships to be seen in the churchyards on the island and those of the other islands off the North Sea coast of Schleswig.

We do not have to go many steps beyond the posts before being reminded that, at this farmstead too, the sea has provided the economic basis of the Rømø islanders' existence. By the sweep well in front of the arched front door, the posts of the garden fence are made of whale ribs, and just inside the front door some whalers' knives hang on the wall. Passing from the passage through a small bed-chamber into the winter living-room facing south

all kinds of maritime objects are to be seen. For example, a skipper's hanging compass suspended from the ceiling has not only made the owner of the farmstead feel at home, it has also been used by him when at sea, enabling him to check the course of the helmsman quickly when resting in his bunk. There is also a model ship in a glass case on the wall, and on the window sill an octant – an instrument for measuring latitude from the height of the sun when on the high seas.

The navigational instruments in the living-room are by no means the sentimental souvenirs of a retired seaman, they are the everyday tools of a ship's skipper to be used on his voyages. It is

The summer living-room – facing north – is next door to the kitchen, a little of the open chimney can be seen through the door. The stove by the tiled chimney wall has been stoked from it.

no coincidence that many farmsteads on Rømø are called *kommandørgårde* or skippers' farmsteads. Many farmers owned shares in ships and captained them, or were skippers for shipping companies at some time or other. The great majority of the male inhabitants of the island, though, were ordinary seamen. Some plied the coastal routes to the south, to Friesland and Holland, but others sailed far greater distances to England, Norway, Sweden and the Baltic countries. It is unlikely that many boats from Rømø sailed to the Arctic and on whaling expeditions; most boats bound on voyages of this nature departed from harbours elsewhere. It became increasingly usual

for seamen of all categories from Rømø to sail on Dutch ships – both cargo vessels and whalers.

Seafaring and whaling brought prosperity to Rømø in the 17th and 18th centuries, particularly the latter half of the 1700's when these activities culminated, to cease abruptly shortly afterwards. Contact with the Netherlands was close during this period. And it is hardly surprising that, among the surviving relics of the old Rømø culture, the building traditions and interior arrangements of the 18th century clearly predominate. Neither is it curious that so many elements of Dutch origin were absorbed by this culture, often with Friesland acting as the intermediary. This island and coastal region was the route between Rømø and Holland, and along its entire length a widespread cultural uniformity developed.

Tiles are the most conspicuous manifestation of the Dutch influence in the home. In the Rømø farmstead at the museum they are found in both the summer living-room to the north, and the winter living-room to the south. In each case the outer walls and chimney wall are covered with tiles. All of them are the usual type with a landscape enclosed in a circle. Those in the winter living-room are manganese coloured while those in the summer living-room have blue motifs. It is a type of tile which found its way in enormous quantities up the North Sea coast in the 18th century. Frilandsmuseet's farmstead is not unique but representative of a very large number of dwellings on Rømø and in the coastal districts of the mainland, all of which were decorated in this manner at that period. The occurrence of several different kinds of tiles in the same dwelling-house is also characteristic. The landscape tiles in the living-rooms are also on the end wall of the gable room, but the tiles round the stove in the summer living-room are decorated in blue with biblical scenes in circles which almost entirely fill the tile they are so large. And in the little chamber off the entrance passage the tiles have been put up in a manganese coloured star pattern.

By no means all the rooms have been decorated with tiles, but their walls are also colourful and festive because the panelling is painted with decorations in many colours. The majority of dwelling-rooms throughout the rest of Denmark undoubtedly had whitewashed walls, only the corner with the table and seating arrangement had to have wooden panelling to protect it from wear. There have, however, been exceptions everywhere in which dwelling-rooms were entirely panelled. Wooden partition walls were very usual, though, in North Schleswig and West Jutland, but in no other area in Denmark is the painted decoration on panelling quite equal to that found on Rømø and the mainland adjacent to it.

The Rømø farmstead at Frilandsmuseet is also the finest example of decorative expression at the museum – folk art. In any event, no other farmstead displays the same wealth of mural decoration in one room after the other. The summer living-room has panelling painted in marbling of blue and bluish-green shades enlivened with touches of red. In the winter living-room there are garlands of flowers on a dark greenish-blue ground. The two large, unheated "best rooms" are dominated by a red shade, against this ground is a profusion of flowers, no doubt particularly appreciated in an environment not endowed by nature with such abundance. On some bluish-green boards and on the ceiling are *rocailles,* the familiar twisted rococo ornament at which the painters of Rømø appear to have become highly practised during the florescence of the island.

Skipper's Cottage From Fanø

The most northerly of the Danish islands off the North Sea coast is divided into two districts: Nordby parish and Sønderho parish. The Fanø cottage at the museum comes from Sønderho. It was acquired in 1913 and re-erected in the course of the next couple of years. The intention was to give visitors to the museum an impression of the dwellings in this special milieu of skippers and fishermen. But it is also an indication that museum circles at that

Opposite page: There is something neat and decorative about cottages on the island of Fanø. The example at the museum also has painted details.

time were beginning to become interested in the construction of old buildings.

For the Fanø cottage can tell us something of interest from the point of view of building traditions and, like the Rømø farmstead, this is best seen on the north side of the building. To all appearances it is a brick "longhouse", but on the north side the uprights of the half-timbering are still visible because timbers on this side have not been exposed to sun and weathering to the same extent as those on the south side. Therefore in order to economise only the south façade onto the road has a faced wall of brick outside the half-timbering. The occupant improved his cottage, while at the same time following the fashion, partly no doubt for reasons of prestige. This feature provides a very good illustration of the transition from half-timbering to brick, and thereby of the general development of rural building traditions in the south-westerly part of Jutland.

But the cottage shows us, first and foremost, how the folk in Sønderho lived in bygone days. There is a little outhouse space at one end: barn, cowshed etc. for the needs of a modest smallholding looked after by the women, or whoever else was home. Fishing has of course been one of the occupations, but the cottage is otherwise most characteristic as the home of a family whose menfolk spent a large part of each year away at sea. The homes of seamen are usually neat, nice and newly painted like a trim ship. Seafarers bring things home and open up links with the outside world. Thus Fanø had a share in the more or less general cultural impulses of the coastal regions up the North Sea coast. The Frisian-Dutch influence is apparent, for example, from the tile-covered walls – both blue and manganese in colour decorated with a variety of motifs, even pictures of ships pieced together by means of several tiles.

Here, too, we find the custom of a winter living-room and summer living-room which was widely adopted in North Schleswig and south-westerly Jutland. The dialect word to describe them is dørns, the winter living-room facing south is sønderdørns and the summer living-room facing north and cool during the summer months is nørredørns. Old people in the region still use the term. The word dørns is a Slavic loan-word which appears to have reached Denmark via Holstein – together with other innovations as regards the interior arrangement of the home.

Lønnestak Farmstead From West Jutland

As is very often the case, Frilandsmuseet knew of this farmstead long before it was possible to acquire it, for already in 1946 during the National Museum's investigation of old rural buildings in West Jutland it had aroused interest. However, the farmstead was not acquired until 1960 and even then, four years elapsed before it was measured and surveyed for removal. It was opened at Frilandsmuseet in the northerly end of the museum park in 1967.

The reason it was re-erected in this part of the museum is partly because there are other buildings near by to which it is closely related, and partly because here the best impression of its native locality could be given. Lønnestak is situated immediately south of Ringkøbing Fjord on the North Sea coast. It is an infertile district. Farmsteads and villages are scattered throughout the arable lands in the most inland part of the parish which drift sand has failed to reach. To the west are dunes that have gradually buried the windswept oaks still concealed behind the more recent fir plantations. In the hinterland extensive tracts of heath alternate with meadow. This is the reason why the farmstead from Lønnestak stands in an isolated plot at the museum, although in its native locality it was part of an open row of homesteads along a road. Its nearest neighbour was the cottage for the retired farmer built much more recently, and at a time when the farmstead was no longer the enclosed entity withdrawn and self-sufficient of former years.

When approaching it from the north road at the museum, it conveys perhaps just this impression of seclusion; a compactness emphasised by the four wings built together in a rectangle turning their backs to the world as it were. But, in fact, this is totally misleading and clearly contradicted by the dwelling-house with its row of windows to the south, opening in a friendly fashion onto the surrounding country. Whether these thoughts were entertained in 1803 when the farmstead was built is doubtful, but they may have had an underlying effect. For its layout was presumably influenced by current fashion, and whether it was followed or not could well have been decided on grounds of prestige. In any event, during the first half of the 19th century a change occurred in the parish of Lønne with regard to the position of the dwelling-house of a farmstead in relation to the outbuildings. The farmstead at Frilandsmuseet is one of the first in which the dwelling-house is the south wing. By the middle of the century only a few farmsteads remained in which the dwelling-house was the north wing with windows looking out onto the courtyard.

In another respect, too, the farmstead was built to open outwards in 1803. The cowshed and stable are different, in that livestock was not herded through the covered gateway into the courtyard to reach their quarters, the entrance to the cowshed and stable was in the outer wall of the wing. By this wall was also the midden, which in other districts was often in the middle of the courtyard. The barn functioned in much the same way, for when crops were brought in from the fields they were unloaded by the outside wall of the barn, and the sheaves pushed through the shutters in the outer wall. Loads of corn were not driven into the courtyard for unloading.

It is fairly characteristic of the Lønne district that the courtyard was a place of little activity and with few functions. But

this may not always have been the case, it may well be the result of an influence from North Schleswig. The Lønne farmstead, moreover, is arranged so that the cowshed can be reached from the dwelling-house without going outside. Again unlike elsewhere in Denmark where courtyards have to be constantly crossed on errands from the dwelling-house to the outbuildings.

The conditions described here apply to the farmstead as it now appears in the museum, and by and large as it was built in 1803. However, in many ways it must have been quite an upheaval for the family moving into this modern farmstead at that period, as it differed in quite a number of respects to what was usual for the district. We know from a map of Lønne parish a little about the appearance of their old farmstead. It was situated a little further into the field, and consisted simply of two parallel wings. Its layout was somewhat similar to the Vemb farmstead at the museum which comes from a more northerly district of West Jutland.

To move from two wings to four must have been a great change, even more so considering the new farmstead was the first in the parish with four adjoining wings. In another respect, as well, the farmer appears to have been a pioneer, for it is presumably the first in the parish to be built of bricks. This method of building gradually spread northwards through West Jutland at a period when all the easterly regions of Denmark still continued building with half-timbering and wattle and daub. In the course of the 17th and 18th centuries bricks became widespread in westerly North Schleswig. The new

A cock pecking in the midden by the Lønnestak farmstead. A cock like this is a great asset at the museum where it enlivens the farmyard by its crowing and fine feathers. The silence of a museum is broken and people feel they are in the heart of the country.

The farmstead from Lønnestak in West Jutland consists of four wings and cannot be seen in its entirety from any one position. This is a view of the south side of the dwelling-house and wing with cowshed and stable. Outside the cowshed door is a glimpse of the midden and dung barrow.

custom had now reached as far north at the beginning of the 19th century as the region just south of Ringkøbing Fjord.

But the plunge from half-timbering to brick was not taken all at once in Lønne either. This can be seen by walking round the outside of the farmstead, for traces of half-timbering have survived here and there in the outbuildings. Archival evidence dating to the first years of the new farmstead bears this out: in two assess-

ments for fire insurances made with a fifteen-year interval, the first immediately after it was built. These reveal that although the farmstead appears to have been built as an integral whole, it has in fact been built in several phases. Originally the wings with outbuildings were of varying breadth, possibly because building material from the old farmstead had been re-used. The second assessment, however, reveals that these irregularities had been rectified, and that part of the half-timbering was replaced by brick.

The dwelling-house, on the other hand, underwent no structural alterations. It was brick built in 1803, the date still to

This is the cowshed at the Lønnestak farmstead. Through the open doors in the background part of a bread oven can be seen.

The courtyard at the Lønnestak farmstead has always been a fairly quiet spot, although water was collected from the well and scythes were sharpened here.

be seen carved into the chimney in the kitchen, and its interior was up-to-date and in keeping with the times in every respect. Its exterior has a hint of the neo-classical style of the period, the harmonious façade with two symmetrical projecting bays, each with a crescent dormer. The interior, too, has features which in older buildings are the result of modernisations. For example, the Lønne dwelling-house has from the very first had a separate kitchen and living-room in the same bay, whereas elsewhere they were both part of one large room.

The living-room off the kitchen also has two alcove beds, and the family ate here by the window, but only during the winter months. A former occupant is recorded as saying that the room was almost to fine to eat in. But the kitchen was obviously too small to eat in. During the summer months the family ate in the scullery.

The two heated rooms in the dwelling-house are the family living-room and the so-called *dørns,* in this case a heated "best room", both were heated by iron stoves stoked from the open chimney in the

196

In the heated "best room" of the Lønnestak farmstead is a noteworthy table, partly because of its length, and partly because there are chairs along the side away from the wall. The door leads into a smaller room which has an American wall clock, an alcove bed can also be glimpsed.

kitchen. The "best room" in contrast to the living-room was not normally used much. It was presumably heated when guests were expected but otherwise not often. Many people could be seated at the long table on fixed benches beneath the windows and at each end by the partition walls, as well as on chairs along the near side of the table. This room is in many ways an interesting one. The tiled chimney wall here and the tiles in the living-room are the most northerly examples of Dutch tiles to have spread as a direct cultural influence along the North Sea coast. The rest of the wall decorations in the *dørns* is noteworthy too, for the plastered walls are decorated with stencil painted patterns, said to have been painted in the 1870's by a local painter called Vind, like those in the second "best room".

The second decorated "best room" came into its own on festive occasions with space enough for dancing and extra trestle tables to eat at. Otherwise the room was mostly used for storing clothing and linen, and its everyday furnishings consisted of chests, cupboards etc. It was not, however, solely members of the family who kept their clothes here. Farmhands and servants also used it for storing their possessions, and each time they wanted to collect something from the room, they had to walk through the entire house. The little room behind this "best room" was used for a time by a farmhand, but it has originally been intended as a guest room. Both farmhands and servant girls had their quarters at the other end of the dwelling-house.

Here part of the scullery has been partitioned off as a small bed-chamber for a farmhand. There is also a larder and bread room – the latter nestles at the outer slope of the bread oven protruding from the open chimney. But the best impression of the size of the bread oven is the way it projects through the wall into a room at the gable used for storing hay.

From the scullery a door leads directly into the cowshed and stable, and this direct access is characteristic of the district. Other details in the outbuildings can perhaps be classified as peculiar to this part of the country. For example, the hencoop above the pigsty is a typical West Jutland arrangement. The modest size of the barn generally illustrates how insignificant cereal farming was in this infertile area.

Peasants had to supplement their living by other means. In Lønne, fishing was one of the most important additional occupations. The Lønne farmstead at the museum has had a share in these fishing activities. It was usual along this stretch of the west coast of Jutland for farming families to settle in huts down by the beach during the fishing season. It is no coincidence that the fishermen's huts at Frilandsmuseet lie so close to the Lønne farmstead, as they have a link with the same parish.

Fishermen's Huts

A little to the north of the Lønne farmstead at Frilandsmuseet is a patch of dunes amid which is a cluster of curious huts. Their position close to the farmstead is intentional. For in the old days the family living there took part in the fishing at Nymindegab by the former entrance of Ringkøbing Fjord just north of Lønne. Here and elsewhere along the west coast farmers moved down to the beach for the fishing season, i.e. in April, May and June. The huts were temporary dwellings used solely during the season. They stood empty for the rest of the year when the occupants returned once more to their farmsteads

Gorse with its armour of prickly leaves grows in many infertil regions. Here it enlivens the dunes with its yellow flowers. There are many species of plants at the museum in order to give an impression of the vegetation of different localities.

The three fishermen's huts are dwellings as can be seen by the chimneys. A fourth not shown in the picture has no chimney, for it was used for storing tools and fishing gear. The hut in the foreground is the original, moved to the museum from Nymindegab in 1910. The chimney is built of turf at one gable by the entrance. Cooking was done at floor level at the base of the chimney. Apart from the wooden gable this seasonal dwelling is a simple roof span set on the ground, thatched with marram-grass collected from the dunes and with a turf ridge.

and cottages further inland, where they lived. The huts therefore illustrate an occupational diversification common in former times.

Huts of this kind became obsolete towards the end of the 19th century, when fishing became a full time occupation. Professional fishermen gathered in communities by the new fishing harbours, while farmers abandoned fishing as a part-time occupation and concentrated on farming. But even in 1910 it was still possible to acquire a fisherman's hut for the museum, although shortly afterwards all trace of them had disappeared. The acquisition is interesting from the viewpoint of the museum's history, in that it was the first building to be acquired and moved from truly Danish territory. This

did not mean, though, that any revision of the principles of acquisition had occurred. The fishing hut was chosen, like the other buildings at that period, because of its strangely primitive qualities. From the criteria of evolutionary sequence it was a good find.

However, it is interesting in other ways because it tells us something about a special form of fishery and the way in which it was organised. In order to illus-

200

Some fishing gear is stored in the hut for tools. Otherwise the only hut to be seen inside is the original one from Nymindegab. The others are copies to illustrate how these huts were always grouped in the dunes. The original hut is equipped in the usual way for this type of hut. At the rear end are two beds, and in front of them a table. The occupants have decorated the upright board behind with wallpaper and hung up some pictures to create a homely effect. Otherwise the interior is impersonal and makeshift as perhaps is to be expected in a temporary shelter.

trate this more clearly, the original hut was supplemented a few years ago by three others, all of which are reconstructions. These have been copied from old measurements, surveys and photographs taken before the last fisherman's hut disappeared from the west coast. The reconstruction was not difficult, as the huts are very simply constructed – a roof span set on the ground and thatched with marram-grass.

The four huts grouped in the dunes at Frilandsmuseet are the exact number to shelter the crew of a fishing boat, an open sea-going craft manned by six or seven men. Two men lived in each hut with their women, whose job it was to bait the lines. This was hard work as fishing was done by a long line to which hooks were attached at intervals with a short cord. After each fishing trip these interminable lengths of line had to be cleaned, repaired, and the hooks baited. The pair of women in each hut also did the housework and cooking. Food was cooked over an open fire at the base of the turf built chimney by the entrance in the gable. Only one of the huts was without a chimney as it was used for storing tools and equipment in.

Farmstead From Vemb, West Jutland

This steading is approached by a long road and can be seen away in the distance long before it is reached. Its situation gives a hint of the heathland of its native surroundings. To one side the heath portrays a region which had until recently many uncultivated tracts of land. The stream just beyond the turf bank enclosing the garden corresponds to that which flowed past the original site. The position of the farmstead close to a stream is of significance, too, for meadows were often the backbone, so to speak, of heathland farming in the past.

Like the other old buildings at Frilandsmuseet, the Vemb farmstead was wrapped in anonymity for a long time, but it was not the removal to the museum which brought it from obscurity. From 1930 until 1960 it had been a museum farmstead in situ, and as such could be experienced in its native environment, in the landscape of West Jutland – on land which had provided successive generations with their living. When the farmstead was acquired by the State in 1930 and therefore rescued from falling into decay, it had aroused considerable local interest and funds were raised in the area which paid towards its restoration. As time passed, however, scarcely any visitors came to see it, and upkeep and supervision became increasingly difficult. It

Previous page: The farmstead from Vemb in northerly West Jutland with a stream in the foreground. On its native site a stream also flowed past the farmstead beyond the turf bank enclosing the garden. In the foreground to the right can be glimpsed the bridge from Smedevad which is also from Holstebro district. The farmstead consists of two detached parallel wings. The nearest is the dwelling-house which also has a pigsty in the gable to the right. Behind is the wing with barn, stable and cowshed.

was then decided to move the steading to Frilandsmuseet, where it would fit very well into the plans already drawn up for the enlargement of the museum. It was dismantled in 1961 and re-opened in 1965 to a far larger public than that which found its way to Vemb. Although the atmosphere of its true setting is absent, it can now be experienced in a historical perspective and compared with old rural buildings from other regions.

The reason for the earlier interest in preserving this farmstead was due partly to the fact that it consists of two detached parallel wings, thus representing a type that was rapidly disappearing, although formerly well represented, particularly in the most northerly third of Jutland. In the Twenties and Thirties a relic of the old-fashioned evolutionary theory still survived in talk of set types of farmstead such as the single wing, the two wing, the three and four wing types. Indeed, during the years before its removal to Frilandsmuseet, it played a role that the farmstead from Vemb was considered primarily to be representative of the special two wing type called the "parallel farmstead". Apart from the small forge of the farmstead (a little distance away and considerably later than the other buildings), the steading consists of two detached parallel wings with a farmyard in the middle. It is almost an illustration of the hall and barn recorded in medieval legislation in Jutland as the most important buildings of a farmstead.

Now a curious fact about the two farmsteads from West Jutland in Frilandsmuseet is that a closer study of their early history confuses former time-honoured concepts. For the four-winged Lønne farmstead originally consisted of two parallel wings before it was rebuilt. While the farmstead from Vemb, on the other hand, the only "parallel farmstead" at the museum is known to have had a

203

third wing before it gained its present appearance sometime in the 1770's. Thus attempts to classify farmsteads call for caution. It has also long been evident, for example, that the amount of land farmed – i.e. the size of the harvest – has influenced the number of outbuildings. But this, too, must be treated with reservation, because corn was stacked outside in ricks in some areas, and when this was done less barn space was needed.

The farmstead from Vemb has had ricks outside the barn, although not presumably in the very old days when the amount of cereals grown in the infertile soil was limited. Hay – an important crop, not least on a heathland farm, also required space. It was not only a question of the amount of cattle which could then be kept, but to a very great extent a question of the dung they provided, essen-

tial for manuring the fields nearest the farmstead.

Heathland farmers also earned a living by other means in the past if they could. Two additional sources of income have meant so much to the occupants of the Vemb farmstead that the means by which they were earned are still evident. Firstly, weaving, a very widespread handicraft among countrywomen except in those areas where there were village weavers – craftsmen in the trade. Therefore, in certain circumstances, the women wove not simply for their own requirements but for others as well in order to earn extra. We see that the small west room in the Vemb

Opposite page: The barn in the Vemb farmstead is a good example of the nave and side aisle construction.

Below: The wood and brickwork of the stable and cowshed in the Vemb farmstead bear traces of many years' wear.

dwelling-house was used by the house-wife for weaving. It is an unheated room, normal for a room principally the "best room" for storing linen and clothing, and used on festive occasions. Here the loom stands, with just enough room for a warping mill – a frame for setting up the warp, and a box from which the warp yarn has led into the frame when the weaving of a new piece of fabric was about to begin.

The other handicraft to provide an extra source of income for the home was the production of so-called Jutland pots. This name did not of course originate in the districts of Jutland where this particular type of pottery was made. It is a name used to describe the ware in some of the areas where it was sold in large quantities. In Jutland they are called "black pots", thereby describing a characteristic of the pottery as opposed to the products of professional potters of the red-fired glazed type. The pots were shaped without a wheel by hollowing and shaping a piece of clay by hand. This was done by the woman on a board in her lap. Unlike the professional potters who were always men, the black pots of Jutland were made by the women. The men of the household only helped to fire the pots, and this process again differed from that of the pottery-making trade. Jutland pots were not fired in a kiln but in an airtight pit fired with heather turf stacked in a special way to keep the air out. Only by this means did the pots turn black. This long obsolete technique leaves few traces behind, and the reason we know that an activity of this kind took place on the heath north of Vemb is because excavations were carried out on and around the site of the farmstead. During these excavations a considerable quantity of black potsherds were recovered, and some burnt patches found – the remains of the pits in which the pots were fired. The only remaining evidence is a circular area of paving excavated at the same time. It is between the barn and the forge, and it has been used for storing the clay for making the pots.

The two existing parallel wings date back to the 1770's but the forge was built about a hundred years later. It was only for farm use, and therefore not a source of extra income but a means of saving, as the farmer could repair his own implements and avoided using the local blacksmith in Vemb. It is undoubtedly situated a little distance from the main buildings because the forge represented a fire risk.

Opposite page: There is a small room in the same bay as the kitchen in the Vemb farmstead. It was originally used as a bedroom, sometimes for the widow of the previous farmer. The old lady could sit here, warmed by the iron stove decorated with an elegant female figure making music. The armchair is made of coiled straw, i.e. thin lengths of coiled straw bound together with osier bands.

Fisherman's Cottage
From Agger

The west coast of Jutland, that is to say the coastal belt and islands of the North Sea coast from southernmost Schleswig to the region north of the Lime Fjord, is fairly well represented at Frilandsmuseet by a range of very different buildings from localities scattered up this long coast. The homesteads span from the largest to the smallest; from the most lavishly equipped homes to be found among the Danish peasantry, to the simplest huts used for sleeping and living in during short periods of intense seasonal work. They represent a wide variety of occupational patterns springing from the interplay of farming, fishing and seafaring.

The most northerly example is the cot-

tage from Agger. It was acquired by Frilandsmuseet in 1923 and opened at the museum in 1925. Apart from the farmstead from the island of Læsø off North-East Jutland which is quite special, the Agger cottage is the only one from the region north of the Lime Fjord, i.e. that part of North Jutland which is in itself an island – severed from the rest of Jutland by the Lime Fjord. It is not entirely satisfactory as the sole representative of a region with fairly marked differences from district to district. But it contains a number of features which are general for this part of North Jutland, apart from those of a more special nature illustrating its adaptation to a particular coastal environment.

At the dwelling end of the Agger cottage the outside wall is set back against the inner uprights to make room for windows. The low outshot has in-fillings of beach stones.

The cottage comes from a corner of the Thy district where the Lime Fjord is closest to the North Sea, thus folk in Agger could fish both in the fjord and at sea. Farming conditions, on the other hand, were difficult. There was never much arable land, and what there has been is now either covered by drift sand or taken by the sea as it eroded the coastline, causing villages to be abandoned. The occupational conditions demonstrated by the cottage at the museum have not only been characteristic of Agger but also of those found in most small homesteads along the west coast of North Jutland. Fishing was the main occupation, but a little farming helped to provide a small

measure of additional economic security. The crops were not impressive, and not surprisingly potatoes when first introduced became an important crop in this sandy soil from an early date, fishermen were thereby less dependant upon the produce of farmsteads further inland. The more prosperous among them kept a few cows, too, and did what they could to fill their small barns with hay. Sheep were widespread in these coastal districts, grazing all the year round on the heathland and among the dunes. They were animals with frugal needs.

Certain details of the cottage both inside and out quickly reveal something about the special conditions of its native district. The most striking feature is the building material in part of the outside walls. Some of the in-filling between the uprights consists of pebbles collected from

the beach, and some of the timber has been salvaged from driftwood. Wreckage and other forms of driftwood were a welcome source of timber in these sparsely wooded coastal areas where a chronic shortage of wood had to be endured.

The construction of the Agger cottage is characteristic of many old rural buildings north of the Lime Fjord, although it has also occurred south of the fjord to the west. The special feature in this context being the so-called nave and side aisle structure, perhaps most clearly seen in the farmstead from Vemb, but also well illustrated in the Agger cottage. Here it is particularly interesting because this method of construction has been adopted in the dwelling end of the cottage. Nor-mally the nave and side aisle construction is more often seen in barns. Only at the dwelling end on the south side of the Agger cottage is the outside wall set back against the inner uprights carrying the roof in order to make room for the windows in the two dwelling-rooms. This lopsided cross-section has been usual in many an old rural building in North Jutland. Another detail occasionally encountered in this region until the close of the 19th century was a chimneyless roof, for we are in an area where the smoke hole or louver survived longer than anywhere else in Denmark.

A block for shaping woollen underpants hangs by the alcove bed in the dwelling-room of the Kølvrå farmstead on Karup heath. It was used for knitwear. Through the door is a glimpse of the kitchen.

Farmstead From Karup Heath

This farmstead, like the Vemb farmstead, attracts our attention from a distance because each of the buildings has a striped roof composed of alternate layers of straw and heather. This curious thatch is a characteristic of heathland farmsteads where straw has been in short supply, and where in any event harvests of long-stemmed rye could not be depended upon. But though cereal crops were small, there was always a plentiful supply of heather which could be used for a variety of purposes, including thatching.

The farmstead comes from Kølvrå on Karup Heath, in the past it was a scattered settlement along the westerly edge of the valley drained by a small river Skiveå. The Kølvrå farmstead consists of three detached wings. Acquired in 1932, it was hurriedly dismantled in 1941 when the German forces of occupation enlarged the military airfield in the locality. It was opened to the public at Frilandsmuseet in 1943.

Its position was typical for a heathland farmstead where meadows by watercourses had to be exploited, for this region is one of the most extensive heaths in Denmark. And heath-like the farmstead unquestionably appears. Outside the timbers of the outer walls reveal the serious lack of wood for half-timbering. Two extreme types of timber are represented. One being the gnarled thin oak from oak scrub

211

A feature which seems especially characteristic of the heathland farmsteads of Central Jutland is the position of the bread oven, situated a little away from the rest of the buildings. From a distance it looks like a small natural mound in the landscape, but on coming closer an opening can be seen. Through this opening the bread oven was stoked with heather brushwood until it became very hot without being of any danger to the farmstead.

Local conditions are also revealed by the interior of the dwelling-house. As is so often the case when a holding was too small or too infertile for a family to live off, an additional means of livelihood was sought. Here, the specialisation was woollen knitwear, for the heathland districts of Central Jutland had a considerable cottage knitting industry. Men and women gathered at the long table in the dwelling-room on long winter evenings to work at their knitting. Blocks were used for shaping woollen underpants and stockings once they were knitted, and one of the menfolk either from this farmstead or another near by left home at periods to sell the goods.

so often a woodland outpost in heathland districts, and also found more westerly here and there conditions permitting. This timber is enduring but the job of fitting it together in a roof-bearing structure is more or less hopeless because of its irregularity. The other type being fir from the stands of fir planted to an increasing extent, particularly during the latter half of the 19th century. This timber is straight and thin, easy to work with but not very durable.

Potter's Workshop From Jutland

This little cottage is among the buildings in the museum which make up the East Jutland village. It dates from the mid-19th century and is the only building in the museum to be built largely of boulders. The façade onto the village street, however, is half-timbered with an in-filling of bricks which is whitewashed like

the boulder walls. The timbers are tarred black. The cottage is also the only building in the museum with a tiled roof. Admittedly it was built with a thatched roof, but this was changed out at an early date because the potter for obvious reasons preferred a less inflammable roofing material, working as he did with a

Opposite page: The potter in Sorring sat on a bench and turned the large lower wheel with his feet. The little wheel at the top of the axle turned in front of him, and with wet hands he shaped a lump of clay on it into a bowl.

The potter's workshop is somewhat different to the other buildings in the museum. Although it once had a thatched roof this was replaced a long time ago by tiles because of the risk of fire. It is also built of boulders, although the façade on the road is half-timbered in the usual way. In some regions of Denmark in the past there have been a number of stone built houses, though most of these are later than the buildings at Frilandsmuseet, and mostly late 19th century. In front of the cottage is a clay pit, a pug mill for kneading clay and trestles for drying the clay ware.

kiln at exceedingly high temperatures.

The cottage was opened at Frilandsmuseet in 1954, having been acquired two years earlier in Sorring, a village more or less midway between the towns of Århus and Silkeborg in East Jutland. The country around Sorring was at one time a centre of pottery manufacture, and during the 18th and 19th centuries a large part of the local population was engaged in it, mostly as an extra source of income in addition to farming. The prerequisites essential for large-scale pottery-making were also present for there was suitable clay in the hills around the village, and plentiful fuel to be collected in the woods of the neighbourhood. Last but not least in this context was the long-standing tradition of pottery-making.

The cottage at Frilandsmuseet is a workshop only. It contains no living quar-

ters, and we must visualise the home of the potter in a small farmstead not far away. Outside the workshop is a pug mill in which clay was kneaded. In one end of the cottage is the room containing two potter's wheels for shaping the pottery, as well as a long brick stove to produce heat for drying the unfired pots stored under the roof. In the middle of the house is the large arched kiln. In the chimney can also be seen the opening of the little lead smelting oven for glaze.

Farmstead From True, East Jutland

The farmstead from True stands at the junction of roads in the museum's East Jutland settlement. It was acquired in True near Århus in 1930, and has been on view to the public since 1942 at Frilandsmuseet. With its size and red-washed walls, it is a striking and festive element amid the other old farmsteads and cottages at the museum. In addition to which, like the other farmsteads of four

The East Jutland village is a colourful gathering of buildings. To the left a corner of the potter's workshop from Sorring. In the centre the shoemaker's cottage from Ødis Bramdrup. To the right the farmstead from True.

wings to be seen here, it is considered by many people to be typical of farmsteads in Denmark.

Although this notion is subject to certain reservations, there is nevertheless a measure of truth in it. As we may expect, farmsteads of four wings are to be found in Scania and Halland, and further north in Sweden are regions where many farmsteads are built round a square courtyard. On the other hand, if we travel south of Denmark, farmsteads of four wings are abruptly left behind, although they are encountered again in certain areas as far away as Central Europe.

In order to answer the question of whether this kind of farmstead is typically

Danish, we must not only consider its distribution outside Denmark, but where and for how long has this type occurred in Denmark itself. We must also determine what exactly we mean by a four winged farmstead. For example, in the farmstead from True the dwelling-house is only separated from the outbuildings by a runnel at each corner, and the three wings of outbuildings all adjoin. Farmsteads built together like this – almost entirely undetached – do not appear to have predominated until after the land reforms at the close of the 1700's. After which the general conditions of farming and technical advances brought about larger crops and more livestock, which in turn required more buildings. Yet farmsteads of four wings have existed before this, although these were not built together they were in principle the same and existed for at least two centuries prior to the land reforms. Caution is excercised in recent research when gauging the type of a farmstead from the number of wings it contains. Possibly the most important factor is that a farmstead of this type is built round a rectangular courtyard, and thus only slightly different to the three-winged farmstead with dwelling-house flanked by two outbuilding wings at right-angles with a square courtyard in the middle.

All this is in some ways extremely well demonstrated by the farmstead from True, for it has undergone a development which demonstrates that we cannot rely too completely on the notion that it has been handed down from generation to generation in its present form. By examining the

timbers more closely, particularly the numbering carved in the timbers by the carpenters before each piece was assembled in the half-timbered structure, it can be seen that each wing has been extended at both ends. In other words, there were originally wide gaps between the buildings. The wing opposite the dwelling-house, though, appears to have been built all at once but, on the other hand, it seems to be later than the rest of the buildings.

We can therefore conclude that the farmstead did not consist of four wings when it was built shortly before 1700 but of three detached wings. It is difficult to judge, however, when the gradual alterations to the original buildings took place, yet here as in so many cases, a little light can be shed on the question with the help of archival material. A description of the farmstead exists from 1809 which shows that at this date the farmstead had its present appearance.

That the buildings of a farmstead changed in shape and size in the course of time is very usual, and a large number of buildings at Frilandsmuseet bear evidence of later enlargements here and there at the ends. Conversely, it is often very difficult to ascertain whether part of a building has disappeared, but this has also undoubtedly occurred. Indeed, a more suitable construction than half-timbering for a structural mobility of this nature is hard to imagine. Building in this technique is – to use a fashionable word – flexible, in that the construction is put up in modules i.e. the unit in a half-timbered building representing a bay. A bay is the section between two upright posts. In a detached half-timbered building one or more bays could be added or removed without undue difficulty and without radically changing the character of a building.

One of the changes in the farmstead

The kitchen-sittingroom in the True farmstead is heated by an open chimney where cooking was done. On the table is a communal beer jug. In the past many dwelling-rooms in the countryside had a jug like this ready for all to drink from.

Previous page: Candles were dipped in the scullery of the True farmstead, one of the many jobs done in the old days in the scullery. In the foreground is a special demonstration arrangement to show visitors how candles are dipped. A ladder rests on two trestles. Across the ladder sticks are placed to which is tied a number of wicks. These are dipped into the tallow cauldron. Each time this is done a little of the tallow sets on the wick, and the candle gets thicker and thicker. Surplus tallow drips onto a piece of cloth put out for the purpose on the floor.

from True can be accurately dated. Yet we cannot be entirely sure whether the rebuilding altered its appearance, although it is not unlikely that several changes were made at the same time. The date 1759 on the chimney above the fireplace in the kitchen living-room gives the year the chimney was built which could well be the first real chimney of the farmstead. Moreover, the chimney is a good example of the type usual in westerly Denmark as opposed to those built in the regions east of Storebælt. The hearth completely fills the base of the open chimney, consequently the person cooking did not stand in it as was the case in Zealand. The extra chimney in the scullery is not either a feature encountered east of Storebælt in Zealand.

The manor-house barn from Fjellerup, northerly Djursland in East Jutland with gateway leading into an outshot along the entire length of the building.

Manor-House Barn

With its heavy, tarred half-timbering, the manor-house barn is almost too dominating in its setting in the most northerly end of the museum park. The low brick buildings of the Lønne and Vemb farmsteads seem to fit into the wide open spaces here far better. It is difficult, though, to prevent buildings of such large dimensions as the Eiderstedt farmstead and the manor-house barn from overpowering their surroundings. However, the trees around them will screen them in time. And as far as the manor-house barn is concerned, it will be less striking when the rest of the manor-house complex is erected. Paradoxically enough, the barn will appear smaller when it is enlarged with adjacent buildings, for it will not

rise up so suddenly and starkly in the landscape.

One may well ask why there has to be a manor-house at Frilandsmuseet at all. And the answer is simply that in order to avoid giving a misleading impression of rural life in the past its social differences have to be represented. At the moment we can see how the farmer lived, and the homes of smallholders, but a significant amount of land in Denmark was owned by estates. Therefore it is important to portray not only the home of the squire, but also the outbuildings of the manor,

Opposite page: Carts in the manor-house barn, also used for transporting large stones. In the middle of the building are the threshing floors divided solely by the harmony of the timber construction.

220

for a large amount of the work of the peasants was carried out here, during the times of labour service on estates before the land reforms.

The roof of the barn is carried by an impressive timber construction: inside the barn are two rows of uprights tied together by two sets of cross beams. Between the rows of posts are the threshing floors and beyond the outer row of posts on each side is an outshot or side aisle. Carts laden with corn were driven into the outshots through the gateway in each gable and unloaded.

The barn comes from the manor of Fjellerup Østergård in Djursland, North-East Jutland. It was acquired together with other outbuildings in 1952, and opened at Frilandsmuseet in 1965. The other outbuildings containing cowshed and stables will be erected at a later date. The manor-house, however, will come from elsewhere.

The Læsø Farmstead

A farmstead which leaves a lasting impression on visitors to Frilandsmuseet is the one from the island of Læsø in the Kattegat. This is largely because of the thick seaweed thatch of its roof, which seems to weigh down the buildings projecting as it does, a long way over the outside walls. When long hair and new music swept the country in the Sixties, all schoolchildren visiting the museum called the farmstead "Beatles' House".

The seaweed roof has been an attraction ever since the farmstead was opened at the museum in 1955 after having been acquired in 1947. These dates apply solely to the T-shaped dwelling-house from Bangsbo in South-East Læsø, and the little post mill close by from Byrum. For a number of years they were the only buildings to represent the island at the museum. And the dwelling-house could tell the tale of the culture of the island, its building traditions, and the seafaring which left its mark on the interiors of its homes. But for all this the dwelling-house was only part of a farmstead, and although seafaring was an important

means of livelihood, supplemented of course by fishing, a certain amount of farming was also done. The absence of outbuildings was a little misleading, and fortunately this deficiency has now been remedied. The museum acquired a barn from Vesterø parish, and a cowshed not far from the native site of the dwelling-house. The barn is not old enough to have had a seaweed roof. After it was re-erected in 1971, the work of putting up the cowshed was delayed because of current difficulties in finding the right seaweed for thatching. The cowshed is older than the barn, and therefore with the traditional type of roof.

Seaweed had many uses in coastal districts throughout the country. It was used for building dykes with and as manure, and particularly for thatching the ridge of a straw roof. Piles of seaweed were also used for roofing huts on the beach, or shelters for cattle in the fields. However, the custom of thatching with seaweed in the present century is hard to find. For example, the last seaweed roof to survive on the island of Endelave in the southern Kattegat disappeared in the 1950's. In the province of Halland, Sweden, a roof of this kind is still to be seen. Obviously Læsø was one of the regions where seaweed was used to a far greater extent than elsewhere in recent times for

Previous page: The gable of the Læsø farmstead under the burden of enormous amounts of seaweed. An anchor chain secures a corner of the roof against blustering winds.

thatching. This is not only because considerable quantities of seaweed were washed ashore but also because the cereal crops on the island were not prolific due to the sandy soil, and therefore the straw not sufficiently long to be suitable for thatching with.

How is a seaweed roof thatched? The procedure is entirely different to ordinary straw thatching. While straw thatch is sewn or tied to laths extending from eaves to ridge, seaweed thatch is only securely coiled round the bottom laths at the eaves and the rest is piled up loosely on the laths. To begin with bundles of seaweed are secured to the bottom three or four laths. These bundles are coiled together like rope where they are secured to the laths. The ends of the bundles which hang downwards are more loosely coiled and spread out. The bundles are tightly packed together along the lath, the gaps are filled with smaller bundles. When this operation has been repeated along several of the laths just over the eaves, a solid shelf of seaweed is made, above which the loose thatch is laid layer upon layer.

Opposite page: The post mill from Læsø is intended for grinding the corn of a single farmstead. From about the middle of the 18th century a large number of post mills were to be found on Læsø.

The dwelling-room of the Læsø farmstead extends through the width of the building. Through the doors can be seen rooms which only extend as far as the middle of the house – the kitchen and bedroom. Behind the whitewashed wall is the open chimney.

It was a very considerable undertaking to thatch a roof in this way, and like so many other big tasks in the peasant communities of the past, thatching on Læsø was a joint operation. Close on a hundred people could be called in to do their share of the thatching. There was a set tradition as to how the participants were grouped into teams, and each team worked under the leadership of a skilled seaweed thatcher. The division of work was clearly defined, and everyone knew precisely what they had to do.

The result was a good durable roof. An ordinary straw thatch normally lasts about twenty to thirty years, a reed thatch slightly longer, and the north side of a roof remains intact longer than the south side. A seaweed thatch, though, may last for centuries. And on Læsø the roofs have proved a valuable source of research as

some very old ones have survived, whereas elsewhere in Denmark it is not easy to find any early forms of thatch. Nevertheless, there are some indications that loose thatch was more widespread in Denmark, and not solely confined to a few islands.

On Læsø, however, not only were some very old roofs preserved, the traditional thatching technique had also continued until fairly recently. When Frilandsmuseet moved the farmstead's dwelling-house it was still possible to seek advice from old people on the island who had helped to thatch roofs with seaweed. Indeed generally speaking, many old-fashioned customs have continued to survive for a long time. This applies to the culture of the

226

The "best room" in the Læsø farmstead is unusual in that it can be heated. The iron stove against the tiled wall comes from Norway. It is a well-furnished room with an alcove bed, it also has an adjoining bedroom.

islanders as a whole, and their building tradition contains other early features apart from seaweed thatch. For example, remains of bole constructions have surprisingly been found, and in the dwelling-house at the museum the north wall under the windows is built partly in this technique with heavy horizontal boards.

Læsø is in many respects what is often termed a relic area, i.e. an area where old cultural characteristics have survived over a long period. Small islands are to some extent isolated and free of the influences which bring about continual change elsewhere. On the other hand, the seafaring traditions of the island provided extremely thriving connections with the outside world for centuries. The

men of Læsø sailed either boats owned by themselves or fellow islanders, or travelled further afield to find employment at sea. It is interesting to note the contrast between backward farming, which the womenfolk had primarily to cope with, and affluent seafaring which brought home impulses and innovations from many parts of the world. The prosperity gained from sailing, trading and a systematic economic exploitation of stranded ships was rarely invested in local occupations such as farming and fishing. Times of affluence appear rather to have left their mark by raising the standard of housing of many of the islanders.

This is also evident in the Læsø farmstead at Frilandsmuseet; the rooms in the dwelling-house have painted panelling and built-in china cupboards. The interior is furnished in the style of the

227

Above: The seaweed roofs of Læsø are not only known as a strange type of roof which can reach a considerable age, and which is of considerable historical interest. The roofs are also the site chosen by many species of flora. The ridge of the roofs were often so broad that they could be used as look-out posts without danger. From the rooftop a good view was obtained of most of the island, especially the beach.

Below: Among the heralds of spring at Frilandsmuseet is the pasque-flower.

period c. 1800 like many other Læsø dwellings, but there are also earlier features in the arrangement of the interior. Moreover, the oldest parts of the buildings themselves date back to 1736. Some pieces of furniture are also earlier than 1800, and the ornamentation on fixtures contains motifs with deep roots in the past. The tall slim pyramids appear to have been a particularly favoured motif on Læsø which often recurs, for example on the sides of the china cupboards. The Dutch tiles round the stove in the "best room" clearly illustrate the influence on furnishing and fittings of lively contacts with foreign countries. In Denmark Dutch tiles have their northernmost limit midway up the west coast of Jutland (the Lønnestak farmstead), and their sudden appearance to the north-east on Læsø is of course due to sea links.

The stove in the "best room" will no doubt surprise the observant reader, as this is not consistent with the earlier description of the "best room" as an unheated room for storing purposes also used on festive occasions. It is a special Læsø characteristic, in that the "best room" was also used as a guest room to such an extent that it had to be a heated room. This is presumably because so many shipwrecked people had to be given shelter, therefore it was more practical simply to let out one end of the house to them while they waited to leave the island. There also had to be an extra kitchen, and perhaps one of the most interesting features of the Læsø dwelling-house at the museum is this little kitchen behind the "best room". For here there is a raised hearth without a chimney, the smoke finding its way out through the louver or smoke-hole in the roof. Even when the "best room" was newly furnished, this must have seemed very old-fashioned indeed to visitors from other parts of Denmark who chanced to see it.

228

The house from Múla is made up of two parts. One end is built of boulder and contains the byre and smoke-room. The other end is of wood and contains the "glass-room".

Buildings from the Faroe Islands

As we have seen, a recurring theme in the preceding descriptions of buildings at Frilandsmuseet has been the creation of realistic settings about them to harmonise with their native surroundings. The houses from the Faroe Islands in the North Atlantic come from an environment which is strikingly alien to most people who visit the museum, therefore it is even more essential to convey an impresseion of the landscape of which they were once part. Without this kind of introduction to the geographical and cultural conditions of the islands, it would be difficult to understand the buildings of a Faroese settlement. It must be admitted, too, that the limits have been reached here as to what can be re-created with justification in this type of museum representation.

Nevertheless, if the buildings are approached from the right direction a little of the atmosphere can be felt of the true Faroese landscape. The best way to gain this impression is to walk up the hill towards it. The path leading to the dwelling-house is very alike the approach on its native site. Or one can walk up the slope towards it as though one has reached it from the seashore. By standing still and with a little imagination, a glance round the immediate surroundings gives a very fair idea of the scenery of the Faroes.

The various small buildings of the farmstead are scattered along the ridge of a hill in the home field above the dwelling-

The smoke-room from Múla was built in 1866 but influenced by a far older tradition. The hearth is in a niche with a special flue. On the floor is a stool made from the vertebra of a whale and a creel with head band. On the bench is a spinning wheel.

house. This field is separated from the outer field by stone walling to keep out sheep and cattle, and to enable part of the inner field to be cultivated. The shape of these patches is curious, they are long and narrow with steps cut between each. This is because the soil was originally worked by spade and, in addition, the strips allowed better drainage in a climate with a heavy rainfall. In the old days a little six-rowed barley was grown, and later a considerable quantity of potatoes, but the primary crop has always been hay.

The chief aim was to provide fodder for livestock apart from the all-important sheep which grazed freely in the outer fields all the year round. The islanders were compensated by the sea and the bird cliffs for the nourishment which the soil could not provide. This high protein diet

could be balanced to some degree by a vitamin C additive in the form of a prolific plant: angelica *(archangelica officinalis),* grown in a small enclosure high up on the slope, the walls of which are made of stones and the skulls of pilot whales.

The dwelling-house stands in the middle of the home field. It was acquired in 1959 in the village of Múla on the northernmost point of the island of Borðoy, the largest of a group of islands called Norðuroyar. In 1961 it was measured, surveyed and dismantled together with the other small buildings acquired at the same time in other parts of the Faroes. They were then

230

shipped to Denmark and re-erected at Frilandsmuseet, where they were opened to the public in 1965. It sounds very easy, but in reality it was a difficult undertaking. Loading the building material from Múla onto a boat was a hazardous venture, for below the site of the dwelling-house (the slope corresponds to that at the museum) was a steep cliff with a c. 60-70 foot drop to the sea. Each bit of building had to be conveyed to the waiting ship by ropeway down the face of the cliff. The undertaking was completed in a few days of eagerly awaited calm – an absolute necessity, otherwise no ship could approach the foot of the cliff. Indeed here, at the so-called "surf cove" no landing was possible for the greater part of the year.

The dwelling-house from Múla is the most important feature of the Faroese farmstead at the museum. The outhouses reveal something about occupational activities, but the dwelling-house is of significance because it tells us something about the evolution of the Nordic dwelling, and should therefore be considered in relation to buildings from different parts of Denmark. Like the copy of the Faroese house at the museum which it replaced after many years, the house from Múla contains both living quarters and a little cowshed. The interesting fact about the former is the difference between the interiors of the dwelling-rooms, one represents an extremely old tradition on the Faroe Islands, whereas the other is considerably later.

It is easy to see from the outside that the house is built in two sections. At one end the thick outer wall is built of stones with turf between, it has no windows. The walls of the other end of the house are of wood, there are small windows in the façade and larger ones in the gable. The stone built end contains the murky "smoke-room" which has neither ceiling nor windows, light seeps through the

Above: Angelica is grown in a little enclosure. A pretty and healthy plant which thrives in moist places like this beside a stream. The little enclosure is fenced in with stones and the skulls of pilot whales.

Below: The watermill from Sandur. By the sluice is a mortar stone for crushing tormentil roots for tanning hides.

The Faroese open-air food store is stone built at the rear and with slats of wood at the front. The slats enable the wind to blow through the building and preserve the meat and fish hanging in it.

louver in the roof. The date 1866 is carved in the timbers by the louver.

This does not seem to be such a distant date compared with the age of a number of other buildings at Frilandsmuseet. And this smoke-room is probably one of the last to be arranged in this way in the Faroes. However, as is so often the case, the actual age is of less interest than the details. When it was built in 1866, it was in many ways influenced by a far older tradition. As the name of the room suggests, the fireplace is of central importance.

The louver in the ridge of the roof lets in the light. With the help of a long pole its opening can be regulated, as the primary function of the louver is ventilation. In the oldest types of smoke-room on the Faroes this had played an important role

because in those days all smoke from the hearth had to pass through the louver. The hearth was originally in the middle of the floor – a natural focal point of the room. However, the smoke-room in the Múla dwelling represents a later stage in which the hearth is situated at one end of the room. There is also a kind of chimney. It is still an open fireplace, but above the square hearth is a wooden cowl which continues as a ventilation duct through the roof.

The smoke-room is an excellent illustration of what a dwelling-room has looked like at a phase of its development which, in Denmark, was largely out-dated in the 16th and 17th centuries. Obviously, we cannot juxtapose the features in detail, partly because the Faroe Islands were influenced primarily by the culture of West Norway and not Denmark in the past. Yet, in the main, parallels can well be drawn within the entire region in which the Nordic house type has predominated.

The basic factor deciding the arrangement of the interior is the absence of windows in the walls. The introduction of windows was one of the great changes to take place in Danish rural building traditions at the close of the Middle Ages. The outer walls of the smoke-room of the Múla dwelling cannot be seen, for a little further into the room is panelling, and the space between the outer wall and panelling is used for alcove beds. In front of the alcoves on each side is a fixed bench along the entire length of the room; these benches were not solely used for sitting on but as a place for putting things. The end nearest the folding table was presumably kept empty as this was where meals were eaten. There were other places to sit as well, for example, a three-legged stool could be moved to the hearth or wherever it was wanted, and another stool made from the vertebra of a whale could also be used everywhere.

The other dwelling-room is arranged entirely differently. This room is called the "glass-room". Light streams in through the windows in the gable, and it is the glass of these windows which has given the room its name. The interior is very unlike that of the smoke-room, it is lit from the side by the windows and not through a smoke-hole in the roof, it has a ceiling because it is not heated by a hearth but by an iron stove stoked from the little kitchen – and free of smoke. The little kitchen is in front of the glass-room, but as most of the cooking has been done in the smoke-room, the kitchen hearth has largely been used when the extension stove was stoked from it for heating the glass-room.

Windows and ceilings were introduced into the Faroes in the 1600's, but only in the more prosperous homes where such comforts could be afforded. At the beginning of the 18th century the families who had windows and ceilings in their homes were still presumably in the minority, but in the course of the second half of the century glass-rooms appear to have become more common. Their advent, however, did not bring about any great changes in the function of the smoke-room. The glass-room remained the "best room" into which visitors to the home were invited. It was therefore furnished with this in mind. In a number of places in the Faroes it was the husband and wife who slept in the beds in the best room, while children and servants slept in the smoke-room. Yet even in households with this division between master and servant the smoke-room was still the general dwelling-room, and the place where most indoor tasks were done.

The corn drying kiln is entirely of stone, and like other Faroese buildings the roof is of turf. Corn was dried and threshed here.

233

The stone standing beside the path beyond the stone wall, separating the inner field from the outer fields, is not there by accident. It is the lifting stone of Múla village which male villagers tested their strength with.

It is also usual for old farms on the Faroes to have some small buildings scattered in the vicinity of the dwelling-house. In places where several farmsteads formed a settlement, some of the buildings were used jointly by the farmers. But this did not apply to the open-air food stores in which mutton, whale meat and fish were hung. It was not unusual for a single farmstead to have several stores for food, e.g. one for meat, one for fish, possibly also one in which wool, skins and fishing gear etc. were stored. A common feature of these stores is that the walls are either entirely or partially made of wooden slats with gaps between to allow the wind to blow straight through the building, thus preserving food for long periods without the use of salt. The open-air food store at Frilandsmuseet comes from Viðarejði on the island of Viðoy, across the water to Múla.

The kiln for drying corn, like the dwelling-house, has also been acquired from Múla on Borðoy. The kiln is situated up the slope from the dwelling, it abuts the stone wall between the inner and outer fields. In a rainy and damp climate such as the Faroese, what little grain that was grown had to be artificially dried before being threshed and ground. Hand mills were usually used for grinding, but sometimes it was done by a little watermill with a horizontal wheel, a splashmill. The Faroese splashmill at the museum comes from Sandur on the island of Sandoy.

Maps etc.

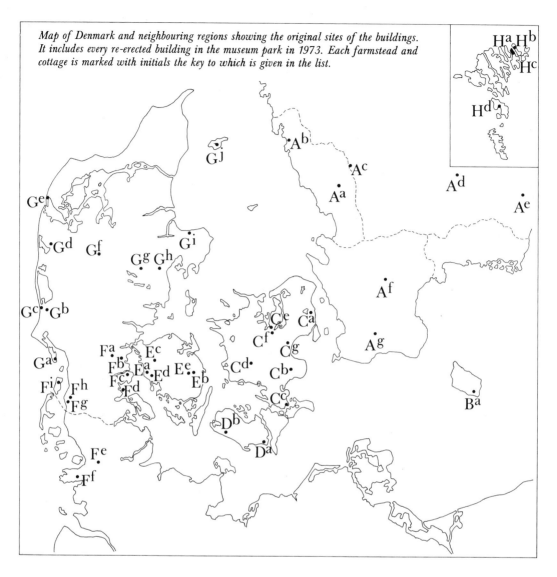

Map of Denmark and neighbouring regions showing the original sites of the buildings. It includes every re-erected building in the museum park in 1973. Each farmstead and cottage is marked with initials the key to which is given in the list.

Halland, Småland and Scania

The Halland Farmstead
    Dwelling-house   A^a
    Outbuildings   A^b
Splashmill from Småland   A^c
Kiln or Bath-House   A^d
The Loft House   A^e
The Näs Twin Farmstead   A^f
The Dörröd Cottage   A^g

Bornholm

Watermill from Bornholm   B^a

Zealand

Fuglevad Windmill   C^a
The Pebringe Farmstead   C^b

Wheelwright's Cottage   C^c
Weaver's Cottage   C^d
Farm Labourer's Cottage   C^e
Fire Station   C^f
Post Mill from Zealand   C^g

Lolland

The Tågense Cottage   D^a
The Dannemare Farmstead   D^b

Funen

The Lundager Farmstead   E^a
Forge from Ørbæk   E^b
The Årup Farmstead   E^c

Clogmaker's Cottage   E^d
Watermill from Funen   E^e

South Jutland
(North and South Schleswig)
Shoemaker's Cottage   F^a
Bole Barn from
    Grønninghoved   F^b
Bole Barn from Sparlund   F^c
Dwelling-house from Barsø   F^d
The Ostenfeld Farmstead   F^e
The Eiderstedt Farmstead   F^f
Farmstead from S. Sejerslev   F^g
Lace School   F^h
Farmstead from Rømø   F^i

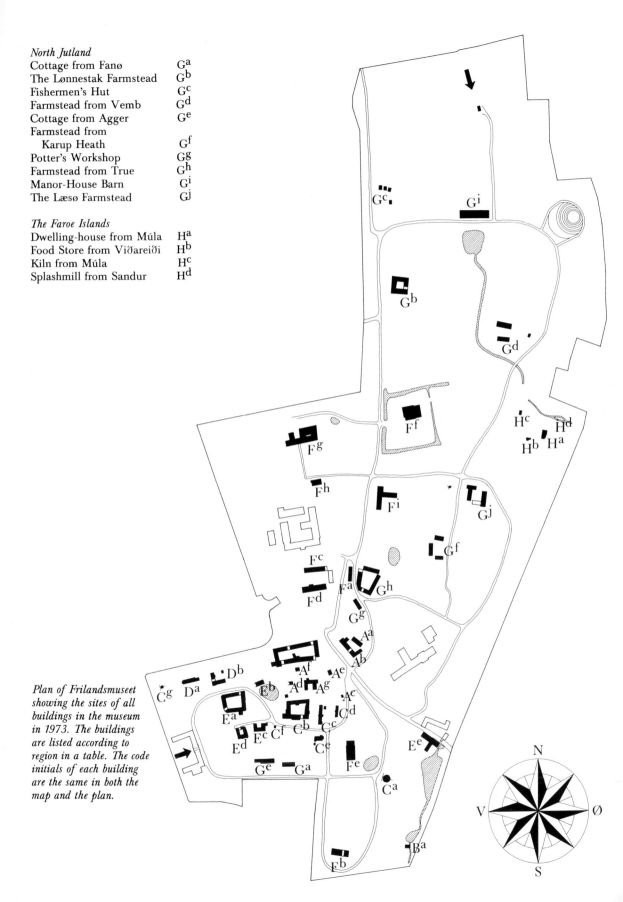

North Jutland
Cottage from Fanø	G^a
The Lønnestak Farmstead	G^b
Fishermen's Hut	G^c
Farmstead from Vemb	G^d
Cottage from Agger	G^e
Farmstead from Karup Heath	G^f
Potter's Workshop	G^g
Farmstead from True	G^h
Manor-House Barn	G^i
The Læsø Farmstead	G^j

The Faroe Islands
Dwelling-house from Múla	H^a
Food Store from Viðareiði	H^b
Kiln from Múla	H^c
Splashmill from Sandur	H^d

Plan of Frilandsmuseet showing the sites of all buildings in the museum in 1973. The buildings are listed according to region in a table. The code initials of each building are the same in both the map and the plan.

List of Illustrations

Original at Frilandsmuseet when not otherwise specified.

All colour photographs are by Lennart Larsen. All have been specially taken in 1972-1973 for this publication with the exception of the interiors of the Dörröd cottage and the Rømø farmstead taken in 1970.

Frilandsmuseet
was printed in offset by I. Chr. Sørensen & Co. A/S,
using Drubin's special inks for matt coated paper.
It was edited by Henning Nielsen, and Jens Lorentzen was in charge of the layout.
Middelboe carried out the reproduction work, and the type used is Baskerville from Askbo.
The paper is 135 g/sq. metre matt coated art paper from Viggo Borch,
and the books were bound by Edm. Jørgensens Eftf. A/S.
Copyright © The National Museum, Copenhagen 1973.

ISBN 87 480 7711 9